Advance Praise for *Going Gypsy*

"Any parents who have gotten through the launc[h] ... sense of adventure (and humor) intact deserve our attention. They got mine! If I could be on the road again—and I guess we really all can—this is how I'd do it. An empty nest just means the kids have learned to fly. How nice to know the parents can too!" —Lenore Skenazy, author of the book and blog *Free-Range Kids*

"It's quite a talent to turn a midlife journey into compelling and amusing reading, and the authors of *Going Gypsy* clearly have that talent. There are as many smiles as miles in this unique travel memoir told in the voices of both halves of a newly nest-emptied couple. Veronica, especially, shares her internal struggle with genuine insight—after all, she's been a *very* involved mother of three kids. Can a couple really just sell the nest and take off in an RV with hardly any plans? Seems so, and we lucky readers vicariously get to enjoy it all with them." —Susan K. Perry, creativity blogger at PsychologyToday.com and author of *Writing in Flow, Loving in Flow,* and the empty-nest novel *Kylie's Heel*

"Warm, funny, clever, and inspiring—makes you see the fun in being empty-nested, whether you take to the road like David and Veronica or stay at home and reinvent your life with the sense of adventure they found on their journey." —Linda F. Burghardt, PhD, author of *The Happy Empty Nest*

"A thoroughly charming account of a romp across America and beyond by childhood sweethearts who discover life without children, rediscover the joy of thirty years together, and learn firsthand the magic of living with eyes wide open to the wonders of a new and independent life." —Victoria Zackheim, editor of *Faith: Essays by Believers, Agnostics, and Atheists*

"As soon as I read the dedication I was 'in,' and the rest did not disappoint. I found myself chuckling at every turn. Loved the writing style as well." —Rayya Elias, author of *Harley Loco*

Going Gypsy

Going Gypsy

One Couple's Adventure from Empty Nest to No Nest at All

David and Veronica James

Skyhorse Publishing

Skyhorse Publishing books may be purchased in bulk at special discounts for sales promotion, corporate gifts, fund-raising, or educational purposes. Special editions can also be created to specifications. For details, contact the Special Sales Department, Skyhorse Publishing, 307 West 36th Street, 11th Floor, New York, NY 10018 or info@skyhorsepublishing.com.

Skyhorse® and Skyhorse Publishing® are registered trademarks of Skyhorse Publishing, Inc.®, a Delaware corporation.

Visit our website at www.skyhorsepublishing.com.

10 9 8 7 6 5 4 3 2 1

Library of Congress Cataloging-in-Publication Data

James, David, 1959–
    Going gypsy : one couple's adventure from empty nest to no nest at all / David and Veronica James.
        pages cm
    Summary: "Ditching the minivan for an RV, one couple embarked on a journey to prove that an empty nest doesn't have to be a syndrome" —Provided by publisher.
        ISBN 978-1-62914-735-2 (pbk. : alk. paper)
    1. James, David, 1959- 2. James, Veronica, 1963- 3. Empty nesters—Travel—United States. 4. Recreational vehicle living—United States. 5. Travelers—United States—Biography. 6. Parent and adult child—United States. I. James, Veronica, 1963- II. Title.
        E169.Z83J355 2015
        910.92—dc23
        [B]
2014014146

Cover design by Danielle Ceccolini
Cover photo credit Nick Coleman

ISBN: 978-1-62914-735-2
Ebook ISBN: 978-1-62914-965-3

Printed in the United States of America

This book is dedicated to our beautiful children, affectionately known as The Piglet, Decibel, and The Boy—our constant providers of entertainment, absurdity, exhaustion, energy, joy, jocularity, and love.

Table of Contents

Everything in this book actually happened. We do tend to remember, and therefore describe, some things more colorfully than others. Many of the names have been changed because we give ridiculous names to most everybody and everything in real life, so why stop here? The chronological order of a few events has been switched around a bit as well, only because we thought it would give the story a better flow.

Before there were late night crying babies, there was us.
Before there were 2 AM feedings, there was us.
Before there were dirty diaper changes, there was us.
Before there were drool-stained bibs, there was us.
Before there were kiss-it-and-make-it-better skinned knees,
there was us.
Before there were school bus stop good-byes, there was us.
Before there were dance classes, there was us.
Before there were Little League games, there was us.
Before there were after-school minivan marathons, there was us.
Before there were junior high school crying jags, there was us.
Before there were prom dresses, there was us.
Before there were nervous-waiting-up-for-them-to-get-home
late nights, there was us.
Before there were tuition bills, there was us.
Before there were graduations, there was us.

Now, there is us again.

Preface

When a twenty-two-year-old beanpole bass player with four years on the road under his belt, and all of the happy hedonism that goes along with that, meets an innocent eighteen-year-old Valley Girl who sneaked into a bar, the ensuing romance is likely to have a shelf life of exactly one night. But somehow that didn't happen.

Even with the eagle-eyed clarity of hindsight, we can't pinpoint the exact reason. It could be that we were all Shakespearean star-crossed. Could be we were both ready for a big change in our lives and just happened to collide. Could be we were just too dumb to know the odds; we certainly didn't set out to defy them.

We are inclined to believe a fourth choice—all of the above. The one-night stand was going on in the next room with the roommate and the keyboard player while we fell into friendship instead of fake, temporary love.

But the road beckoned, and the band had to be back in Nashville, so that was that. Just two ships passing in the night. No one would ever know what might have been.

But that wasn't that. Through the magic of pen, paper, envelopes, and stamps, they kept in touch. The Beanpole wrote to his new blue-eyed beach baby friend because something told him that couldn't be that. A voice was whispering in her ear too, so The Valley Girl wrote back. Before long, an old-fashioned, long-distance romance developed, almost entirely through the US mail. She says she fell in love through those letters. The Beanpole was already there when he started writing.

A few months later, fate—and a good bit of specific action seeking a band working on the West Coast—brought The Beanpole back to California for a face-to-face reunion. With this open-ended employment in the Golden State, young love had time to take its course.

Our story took a less fairy tale–like turn from there. The gig fell apart. What followed was a two thousand mile trek back to Music City in a $200 land barge named The Sharkmobile that had no reverse and no air conditioning, then a brief cohabitation and a "We ought to get married," "Okay," engagement. The next thing we knew, we were in the middle of a folding chair–bedecked wedding in a tiny, windowless, tile-floored church basement. Not exactly the groundwork for happily-ever-after.

* * * * *

The odds of any marriage reaching ever-after are about fifty-fifty at best. Add to that a teenage bride and a road musician groom, then multiply that by being dead broke, and Veronica and I certainly seemed doomed. Good thing no one told us.

Before long we were calling our parents from a pay phone (our home phone had been shut off due to lack of funds) to tell them that they were about to become grandparents. I have often wondered what they must have been thinking.

Back when that beanpole bass player met The Valley Girl's father, right before they ran off together, I remember being intrigued by the lack of any shotguns involved. But then, her dad did have an old hippie vibe about him. Old? He was a lot younger than we are now.

Even meeting my future mother-in-law went well. My new love wasn't living at home, so I guess I wasn't officially robbing the cradle, but still I expected to get grilled. Didn't happen; Mom took right to me. Her stepfather didn't say much at all.

By the time we were expecting their first grandchild, I had won over Stepdad, and we were joking that Mom liked me better than her own daughter.

As for us, few things can motivate reasonable human beings like the prospect of parenthood. We went with stunning velocity from laying around the love nest to up off our asses. Suddenly we were responsible for a life other than our own. We began to form tangible long-term goals.

In time, two more little ones arrived, and we learned that busting butt is what parents do. Find a way. A mother of three could start a company in her home because she learned how to make websites before most people had even heard of the Internet. A dad could successfully navigate a path in an occupation that regularly leaves the crushed carcasses of marriages and families in its wake.

Life's twists and turns took us from Nashville to the Virgin Islands, always in search of the best situation for our family. In general, we met our goals but realized that they revolved around getting the kids raised and started on their own lives. That is the short story of how, after twenty-some-odd years, we found ourselves living on a tropical island in the Caribbean about to become childless again, and wondering what to do.

We didn't have a clue, but somewhere in the recesses of our brains we must have known that the time had come to do something just for us. I know that sounds selfish, but any parent knows that once the kids arrive, there's not a lot of room left for the "us" in a couple.

And our time arrived way ahead of schedule. Let's just say that Veronica and I prove that even the best forms of birth control are only 99 percent effective, but in hindsight we wouldn't have had it any other way. We had the stamina to survive three little ones back then, and now they're full-grown and we're still young enough to enjoy our new life together.

That was our answer. That was what to do. Rediscover that prekid couple who, thirty years ago, didn't have enough time together. Because now, we had all the time in the world.

This is not a "how-to" book or a self-help manual. We would never presume that anyone should do things the way we have. It's simply the story of our journey.

1
Life after Kids

By the time our youngest, The Boy, was finishing his senior year of high school, we had already sent his two older sisters successfully off into the world. We knew the drill. That's not to say it was easy to see them go, but our pride in them and their desire to start their own lives far outweighed the melancholy. The Piglet and Decibel have both thrived outside the nest.

Perhaps I should give some explanation about those names. Our eldest, The Piglet, has just always been The Piglet. I don't remember how it stuck; it may have been a Pooh thing. But even now, as a big-city journalist, she will answer to it. If she minds, she has never let on. Sometimes she even refers to herself as such.

Decibel, on the other hand, is self-explanatory. It's a volume issue. She is loud and impossible to ignore . . . always has been, always will be.

Their leaving brought a flood of bittersweet emotions, hopes, and fears. But each time, there was the task of finishing up with younger siblings. We still had work to do.

This time it was different; there would just be us after The Boy took flight. We were ready to seriously ponder what our life after raising kids would be. This was an opportunity. A chance to celebrate, reconnect, and live a little, but we had yet to determine exactly how.

One lazy St. Croix Saturday morning, we were lingering in bed with the tropical sun streaming through our window. Veronica was reading a paperback, and I had laptop in lap and gears turning and grinding inside my pea brain. There may have been a small puff of smoke wafting out of my right ear. It had popped into my head to Google "empty nesters."

I wanted to see if anyone else was looking at this stage of life from a point of view like ours. *We've spent twenty-five years raising kids. Isn't*

*it great that they have grown up, moved out, and started their own
lives? We'll have our time to ourselves again.*

After typing into the search box and hitting enter, I said, "Look at
this, honey."

The biggest item on the first page was an enormous ad for an Alzheimer's patch.

Veronica's response?

"Holy crap! What's wrong with these people? We just finished raising our kids; we're not dying." Ah, she was engaged now. "Keep looking. Let's see what we can find."

So I did, with Veronica ditching her book to look over at my screen
more and more. Soon my quest had become a joint effort. All we could
find were websites that lamented how terrible it was that the kids weren't
around anymore. A lot of self-help, self-absorption, and self-pity.

Raising kids is hard work, and we couldn't comprehend all of these
people grieving the end of the task. Granted, continuation of the species
is one of life's most important activities. But unlike the other critters on
earth, once we have finished the job of rearing the offspring, we're able
to have some fun. To accept a big pat on the back. Job well done.

The kids have grown into full-sized Homo sapiens fully capable
of feeding themselves. The time had come to let them do their own
hunting and gathering. When they get hungry enough, they will find
food. But they have to learn to do it for themselves. Otherwise, they'll
end up like zoo animals. When tigers get fed every day, they never learn
to hunt. If they're released into the wild, they starve.

Personally, we taught our little cubs that if they get really hungry,
they can always kill and eat a bag of ramen noodles. They've gotten
pretty good at it too.

But we had barely evolved into full-grown human beings ourselves
when Veronica and I started having babies. While many people our age
were still in school, we were raising kids. Veronica transformed from
child to mother while I figured out that Daddy better get off his rump
roast and bring home the bacon. For my work, that meant hitting the

highway. As a general rule, we musicians have to go to the people—they don't come to us.

As with almost everyone else of our generation, it took the combined incomes of both parents to bring home enough pork product to raise three kids. Because of the logistics of road work, the bulk of the child rearing landed on Veronica's shoulders, so she, like so many other women, juggled work and mommying with the skill of a circus performer. She took on various jobs—waiting tables, delivering pizzas, even watching other people's kids, all while tending to our ever-growing brood. Sometimes I could swear I heard calliope music.

Meanwhile I was away from home 250 to 300 days a year as a traveling troubadour in a never-ending hillbilly roadshow. And through it all, Veronica and I always tried to remember that a huge part of being good parents was being a good couple.

In a weird way, all of the travel may have helped our fledgling family. The money certainly didn't hurt, but the constant emotional goodbyes and happy homecomings managed to keep our relationship fresh. Sometimes absence does make the heart grow fonder.

Through the years we worked out our lots. I found ways to travel less and still keep the wolf from the door, while Veronica started a home-based web design business that allowed her to grow into her helicopter mommy self.

As our Spawn grew, the parenting became more of a joint venture. By the kids' teenage years, we were both fully engaged. We had to be, because raising teenagers requires all hands on deck.

Having survived the terrible teens, we had any number of conflicting feelings, and these days even the smallest emotion or complaint must be labeled as a syndrome. It was right there on my computer screen, in bold type: **empty nest syndrome**.

How in the hell can kids moving on with their lives be a syndrome? Shouldn't that be like *breathing oxygen syndrome*? Shouldn't we be excited about this portion of life? Most of us have made more than a few sacrifices to get here, so we say stick a fork in us, we're done. It's not only *not* selfish to take a little time out for ourselves after surviving three teen-agers; it's insane not to.

While clicking onto page after page of empty nest lamentations, an idea began to germinate. A plan to have no plans. Veronica and I could be the kids for a change. The time had come to get back to just the two of us, to resurrect what brought us together in the first place. We could cut loose and go wherever we wanted, be untethered and free. Wander the globe. Veronica could finally see all of the places I'd seen while singing for my supper. We could Go Gypsy. Gypsy Empty Nesters. GypsyNesters.

The theory sounded great in my head, but in real life there were logistics to being footloose and fancy free. We would have to untangle ourselves from all of the possessions and responsibilities that held us down. We couldn't travel by telekinesis and would need lodging of some sort along the way. These things require funding and a modicum of preparation.

While I babbled on about these ideas, my mind was beginning to formulate some viable modi operandi. Veronica's mind, however, was going in an entirely different direction.

Could a homebody mommy who's been totally engaged in her kids' lives really just cut and run? I think her inner voice might have been whispering, "What are you thinking?"

2
Fear Conquering

David made it sound so simple, but after I took a little time to think about it, I had to confess to some anxiety concerning this GypsyNester stuff.

It didn't help that most of the family and friends to whom I'd mentioned the plan-is-no-plans idea found it harebrained. Frankly, I'm not quite sure it wasn't.

I'd become a bit of a worrier over the years (okay, a lot of a worrier) and had morphed into quite the homebody. I wasn't convinced that homebody was my natural state, or even what my natural state was at that point. I'd liken it to my hair—I've dyed it for so long, and in a rainbow's worth of different colors. I'm not really sure what would come out of my head if I let it grow without intervention.

The cold hard fact was that my kids had become my life. I'm not the first person to say this—but I'm not just saying it. My purse became a diaper bag. My car became a minivan. My me-time became their-time. I even sold my thriving web design business in Nashville and took a job at their school when we moved to St. Croix. When I called myself a helicopter mom, I wasn't kidding. No one hovered like me. My rotor blades were sharply honed.

My job at the school, which had begun as designing their website in exchange for tuition, became a rewarding career involving all of the school's technology systems. My best friends were my colleagues—The Spawn's teachers, deans, and advisers. I was entrenched.

By working at the school, I probably knew *way* too much about what was going on in my children's lives, but I wouldn't have had it any other way.

I knew all of their classmates by name. Some of these kids even came to me to sob on my shoulder, tattle on The Spawn, share dreams and goals, or just hang out to have a laugh or two. I was their room mother in junior high, mother-confessor in high school, and the one they begged to go to Chicken Shack for after-school SAT prep session snackage. They brought their lists of prospective colleges to me, seeking my opinion of their choices, and excitedly stormed my office when the acceptance letters arrived.

The idea of The Boy and his classmates moving on and leaving me behind at my desk was heartbreaking; I wouldn't be able to bear it. It was time for me to move on as well. I just needed guts.

Could I give up my home and embark on an undefined mission? When I think back to The Beanpole and The Valley Girl, and their willingness to take life as it was thrown at them, I can still feel the excitement of it all. The joy of new love, the world before us, tethered only to each other. We were broke and naive, yes, but we were free—and fearless.

I needed to believe it was possible to become like that again, to return to what David used to call it, our Nation of Two. A magical land with closed borders and no foreign policy. A realm where nothing and nobody outside its boundaries mattered. A country with only two citizens, a Nation of Two. The blissful State that Kurt Vonnegut so eloquently proclaimed in *Mother Night*.

That's the place—if we could find it again—where we could shut out the world and reconnect as a new childless, or more correctly—as much as I hate the term—empty nest couple. A more stable and smarter version of what once was.

I was not that fearless young girl anymore, not by a long shot. Motherhood knocked her right out of me. Fear was my constant companion. I feared for my children's safety, but my concerns went way beyond any normal mommy protection instincts of diseases, injuries, accidents, afflictions, or tornadoes in Tennessee and hurricanes in the Caribbean. No, I took it to the level of solar wind and magnetic storms. I stressed about the prospect of massive meteor strikes, volcanic eruptions, and tectonic shifts in the earth's crust. What if the world spun wildly off its axis? I anguished over nuclear annihilation and possible alien invasion.

Was Soylent Green really people? It got to where I was even afraid of zombies terrorizing the neighborhood. I was a big sloppy mess of fears.

Then, for the first time, I started to fear the world's perception of me. I not only needed to be the best mother in the world—I was terror stricken that I wouldn't be perceived as such. I was mortified by every mistake I made, beat myself up when things didn't go right, and I replayed anything that could possibly be seen by the outside world as less-than-perfect child rearing over and over in my head.

The more I reflected on these things, the more I realized that I had some serious issues to deal with. This had to happen soon if we were going to abandon our island home and wander the world.

So, in an attempt to alleviate my apprehension for the unknown and scary, I decided to take a self-defense course. I saw huge growth potential there. I wanted to be able to protect myself from what lurked in the dark alleys of my mind.

My friend (and The Boy's biology teacher) Kate was on board with me, which was great because when Kate gets on board about something, she gets balls-out on board. Kate's husband, a karate guy (and The Boy's chemistry teacher), knew of a class at his dojo, so he signed us up.

Beautiful, slight, middle-aged Alda was our class instructor. My first reaction was *gimme a break, even I could kick her butt. How can this woman teach me to be brave?*

We started off with some breathing exercises, and Alda explained that the first line of defense for any woman is to run away. This made perfect sense to me—by nature I'm not a hitter; I'm a runner. We worked on body awareness, muscle memory, and strengthening exercises. We talked about trusting our instincts and keeping our cool. That was good, that was very me. I could do that.

But that Alda chick was a wily one. As the class progressed, I learned some surprising (and slightly disturbing) things about myself.

At one point I found myself looking down at Kate in stunned confusion after throwing her to the mat in a rapist-repelling maneuver.

The objective of this exercise was to learn to use the momentum of the defensive maneuver to spring to our feet and run like crazy women.

Running was not what my adrenaline-charged brain and body wanted to do at all, though. What I *wanted* to do was rush at my fictitious rapist and kick him in the face. How *dare* he treat me like a victim! Luckily for Kate, I decided that kicking her in the face was not a nice thing to do. I do have manners, after all.

Being the pacifist (wimp) that I am, I was in total shock that I could have such a violent reaction to a circumstance that would normally turn me into a puddle of melted Jell-O. This was not the growth I had expected, and I didn't know I had it in me. It rocked.

My confidence grew. Maybe I *could* try new things and step outside of my comfort zone. And knowing how to kick a little butt couldn't hurt if the need should arise.

On the drive home, I resolved to begin a project I'd been putting off for a while. Rockin' my new confident self, I strutted into the house, a woman on a mission.

I dug out a desk calendar and a red magic marker; the time had come to officially commence the countdown. I wrote cheery notes to myself on each day of the week leading up to June 8, The Boy's Dreaded Graduation Day.

"Keep your chin up!"

"Thirty days 'til freedom!"

"Your ovaries may be dead, but you're not!"

I deserved this dirty little secret. I'd spent a quarter of a century raising The Spawn. I'd gotten all three of the buggers to maturity alive and relatively unscathed—it was high time I started celebrating a job well done. A new and exciting chapter in my life was about to begin, and by God, I was going to look forward to it—with as little guilt as possible. I'm a fairly guilt-based person. I was raised Catholic, so it's in my DNA.

For The Boy's sake (and to avoid horrified looks from house guests), I would keep the calendar under the mattress and yank it out first thing every morning to cross off another day, like a jailbird awaiting parole.

It occurred to me that this new outlook would not make me impervious to emotional milestones along the way. I glanced over at The Boy's graduation announcement, emblazoned with his cap and gown photo. My heart almost stopped when I saw it. I had spent many moments in the privacy of the bedroom staring at it and bawling, wondering how my baby got so big.

Learning from prior graduation debacles, I knew that it paid to plan ahead if I wanted to avoid public emotional outbursts. The Piglet and Decibel might never forgive me for the coyote-like howling from the coveted front row aisle seat at their graduation ceremonies. So I markered in "Convince Dr. Feelgood to write happy pill prescription" on June 1 and "Sleep like the dead" on the boxes for June 5, 6, and 7. I added to the June 8 box:

Do not sit in the vicinity of these people

1) Other mothers graduating their youngest child

2) Single mothers graduating their only child

3) David

The school community at large would thank me (I'm kind of notorious).

I wrote in similar notes for The Boy's last Tuesday with us, the last macaroni and cheese dinner, his last dentist appointment, and, of course, the last time he'll throw off his shoes and socks in the middle of the living room floor (another June 7).

As I knelt down next to the bed to tuck my crutch safely into its hiding place, I prayed that my newfound resolve would hold.

3
When Hurricanes Blow

As much as Veronica's prison countdown calendar seemed to help her cope with the last chick flying off from our nest, I couldn't help but notice that her marking off the days was harboring a small boatload of denial. She had circled The Boy's high school graduation as her release date, as if there wasn't one last major undertaking awaiting. Her helicoptering self had been fully engaged in the process of selecting a college, so she knew full well what was coming. But just as with the girls, the mother in her was bound to struggle with the finality of actually sending The Boy off to his new life. It would be the last flight of the helicopter.

She had avoided some of the sting of good-byes with the girls by sending me with them when they left for school. That way she could stay home with the remaining siblings and still be mommy. But this time, she would have to find her solace somewhere else. I hoped that somewhere else would be the sanctuary of our Nation of Two, pride in our offspring's accomplishments, and in our role as parents of adults. After all, we weren't through being parents, just through being parents of children.

During The Boy's transition we would still be involved in his life and education, and certainly affected by his decisions. There were some valid concerns. Would this be the right college for him? A good fit? A place where he could thrive and hopefully excel? Would he get there all right, or could there be another stormy adventure like Decibel's? There was no way of knowing until after the fact.

We did have the comfort of knowing that our excursions into the university admissions process had worked out well so far, even if not always as planned. The kids had taken the task extremely seriously. Choosing a school was the biggest decision they had ever made. We feel that each time the final result was the proper match between school and student, even if there were some storms along the way.

All three prospective students had been very good about pursuing scholarships, taking the tests, making their lists, and submitting all of the proper paperwork. Each eventually chose the respected school in their desired field of study that made them the best scholarship offer. Even though those offers never came from the college that was their first choice, they ended up in very good schools and understood the finances involved.

We had made a deal with our kids well in advance. They would give us one thousand dollars toward tuition, and then we would pay the balance and their housing expenses. Everything else was their responsibility. They had all saved up before heading off, and then found jobs to cover their food, books, and spending cash. We felt strongly that it was important for them to have a financial stake in their education, as well as not bankrupt their parents. They all agreed and made their college selections accordingly.

Ultimately, through fate and possibly an act of God, I am convinced that each of our scholars ended up with a better experience at these runner-up schools than they would have at their initial favorites.

The Piglet had her hopes set on going to New York City but got a huge scholarship award from a Washington, DC, school that gave her opportunities in broadcasting she probably wouldn't have had in the Big Apple. Now, after a great education, she lives in Manhattan, just like she pictured it.

Decibel's best offer came from Tulane University in New Orleans, not the exclusive theater school she had dreamed of, but she gladly accepted. We were thrilled—a great school in a great city. However, she never attended a single class there.

In late August of 2005, Decibel flew up to New Orleans to embark on her college career. Just as I had done with The Piglet, I tagged along for moral support, for a couple of last good meals, and to break out the credit card for the stuff she'd need to get settled into her dorm. One last weekend with Daddy's Little Girl.

That time of year is the heart of the hurricane season, and we lived on an inescapable island on the buckle of the Atlantic Basin's hurricane belt. We had learned to keep a close watch on every storm, so we had been following Katrina since it was a tropical depression off the north shore of St. Croix. All of the forecasts had it headed for Florida, and we boarded our flight confident that everything would be fine in Louisiana. But we had also learned from experience that those predicted paths are subject to change. And change it did. By the time we checked into our hotel in New Orleans, the clerk handed me this nugget of news along with our key.

"Looks like we got a storm comin' right at us."

"No, it's gonna hit Florida, isn't it?"

"Nope, they moved it. I just saw it on The Weather Channel. Turn it on when you get up to the room."

Sure enough, that mother was coming right at us. This was Friday night, Decibel's registration and orientation were the next day, and she was getting a little nervous. But it was late and we were beat, so all we could do was wait and see what it looked like in the morning and decide what to do then.

Early Saturday, Katrina was still coming right at us, up to a category three now, a little over a day away from landfall.

"Let's go get you checked in, then come back here and see about getting out of here before it hits."

I could see the disappointment on her face. Decibel had been chosen from all of the incoming musical theater students to perform a vocal solo at the orientation ceremony, and she really wanted to do it.

"Maybe they'll still have the ceremony, honey. Let's go over and see what's going on."

What was going on shocked both of us. No one was acting like anything out of the ordinary was looming. Just a typical welcome-to-college morning, with long lines of excited freshmen registering and the football team, sporting their kelly green jerseys, helping kids carry their stuff up to their assigned dorm rooms. Go Green Wave. Nobody seemed to think that this was anything more than a pleasant late summer day. Decibel lost it.

"Don't you people realize there's a huge hurricane coming this way?" came flying out of her mouth at the top of her lungs.

We don't call her Decibel for nothing.

The Caribbean kid couldn't believe what she was seeing. By the time a hurricane was a day away from us in the islands, we had boarded up all the windows, laid in several weeks' worth of supplies, and battened down every hatch that could be battened. There is no choice but to hunker down. It's not like we could drive away. But here, there were no visible signs of preparation, and not just at the school—the whole city seemed oblivious.

I was confused by this lack of concern, but not confused enough to get caught up in the nonchalance. I told Decibel I didn't think we should put any of her stuff in her dorm room. She agreed. It was on the sixth floor, with a big picture window overlooking the quad. Great room, but not for riding out a hurricane. We both knew that window was toast. Everything stayed in the trunk of our tiny rented car.

Decibel really wanted to hang out on campus until the orientation at two o'clock. It was nearly noon. I convinced her to come with me back to the hotel. The last thing I wanted was for us to get separated.

"We'll come back for the ceremony."

She reluctantly agreed. Driving across town, we saw that the roads were starting to fill up, and every gas station had a line several blocks long. At least some people were planning to leave, but that looked to be the sum total of any preparations. From the hotel, I called our airline to see about getting tickets home. That wasn't going to happen, as everything was full or canceled, along with the trains and buses.

I have never been so happy to have a rental car, because there was no other way out of town. The best option seemed to be to go north, inland, away from the storm. My brother and his family live in St. Louis, and a quick call to my sister-in-law confirmed what I already knew: her casa was our casa for as long as we needed it to be. But first we needed to find out what the school had planned.

"Let's go see what's going on at orientation, then we can leave right after that."

That brightened Decibel's face up a bit. Maybe she would get to sing after all. When we arrived at the auditorium there was a fair amount of confusion. Unlike earlier in the day, when no one seemed to have a care in the world, news of the impending danger seemed to have made the rounds. Before Decibel went up to the stage I told her that I would be waiting right by the exit.

"As soon as you finish singing come straight back here so we can get the flock out of here."

She nodded and headed for the stage. From my spot by the door I watched my daughter climb up on stage and talk with the dignitaries. I really wanted her to get to perform. My daddy heart was beaming with pride, but just when it looked like she might get her moment, the university president took the microphone.

"An evacuation has been declared. Anyone who has transportation should leave immediately. If you do not have transportation please stay here. We have buses coming to take everyone to safety."

That brought about some minor chaos in the hall, but Decibel fought her way back to me. I felt horrible for her. Her little teenaged heart was crushed. All I could offer was the hope that they would do the program again after the storm.

By now the city was taking on an ominous tone. Even Decibel felt it. Lines at the gas stations were nearly a mile long. Luckily we picked up our car the night before with a full tank. The freeways were completely jammed. Police were everywhere. An air of urgency, with a dash of chaos, had taken hold.

I figured we'd better grab some stuff at a store. Even though I was not thrilled at the prospect of wasting several hours fighting a crowd, it looked like we would be stuck in our car for quite a while, maybe all night. We were once again shocked by the lack of preparations. The huge windows of the supermarket were not being covered, and the surprisingly small amount of customers inside were only buying handfuls of items. The lady checking out in front of us with one gallon of water and some Vienna sausages said to me, "The power will just be out for an hour or two." I hope she made it through.

By the time we got out of the store, the police had announced contra-flow lanes for the highways. With all traffic, in all lanes, on both sides of the highway being directed outbound, insanity was prevailing on the roads. This was anybody who's ever held a steering wheel's worst nightmare. An entire major metropolitan area was trying to drive out of town, all at the same time, on just three or four highways.

The ninety miles to the Mississippi border took us over eight hours to cover. That's at an average of less than twelve miles an hour. I had plenty of time to figure that out in my head while we creeped along. The next hundred miles were a little better—we made them in five hours or so. Then it began to clear out a little, but there were still no vacancies at any of the motels. Finally, with the Sunday morning sun coming up, we found a funky little place in Arkansas and collapsed. Later that day we got back out on the road to St. Louis. By the time we made it up to my brother's place, the storm had pounded the Gulf Coast.

On Monday, Tulane was still planning on opening in two weeks. New Orleans had dodged the worst of the storm and the levees hadn't broken yet. We decided to fly back home, and then Decibel could come back up on her own in a couple of weeks. I called the airline, and they were very helpful about arranging our tickets.

The only thing left was to turn in the car. Obviously I couldn't return the car to the office where I had picked it up, but the company was nice enough to waive the one-way drop-off fee. That was quite swell of them since their vehicle would have been destroyed if it had stayed in New Orleans. However, drop-off fee or not, they didn't have an office in St. Louis. They informed me that I could return the vehicle to either Chicago or Kansas City, or just keep paying for it until their office in New Orleans reopened.

I had already booked our flight from St. Louis, leaving that evening. Damn, should have called the car place *before* I booked the tickets. The best option I could come up with was to drive to Chicago, turn in the car, and get my exhausted ass back to St. Louis in time for a 6 PM flight. It was 10 AM. No problem.

The highway was still full of people fleeing north from Katrina, but I picked my way through the traffic and made it to Chicago in pretty good time. I was working well with my combination of adrenaline and sleep deprivation, clinging to just the proper mixture of caffeine and frantic.

The only thing left to slow me down was security at the airport. I can't imagine why anyone would ever want to get airport security's undivided attention, but if they did, looking completely frazzled while running furiously for a flight, with no luggage, and a one-way ticket purchased right before take-off does a fine job of it.

I was pulled out of every line, sent into special booths, quizzed, grilled, questioned, and interrogated at every possible checkpoint. Luckily, I never heard that butt-scrinching snap of a latex glove going onto a hand, and I had a good story. I think they might have even felt a little bit bad for me. But that didn't stop every single person I talked to from marking up my boarding pass. By the time I used it to actually get on the plane, it looked like a tic tac toe game where both players used red markers.

My brother had Decibel waiting for me at the St. Louis airport, and we caught our six o'clock to Puerto Rico with seconds to spare. It was in San Juan, waiting for our puddle jumper home, where we first saw the devastation from the broken levees on CNN. Decibel was beat, emotionally spent. Me too. All I could do was state the obvious.

"I'm sorry, honey. I don't think you're going to Tulane."

And she never did.

Within a few days we were blown away by how many universities stepped up to the plate and were willing to take in students from Tulane, no questions asked, even forgoing tuition. Decibel tried her sister's school in Washington, DC, for a semester, but unlike The Piglet, hated it. She transferred to a small theater school in New York City.

There's no way to know whether this situation resulted in a better life experience for her than four years at Tulane would have, but I think it did. I can say this for certain, though: I am proud of her coming through the episode and embracing her new path. All at the top of her lungs.

Meanwhile we learned a valuable lesson about sending a kid to college. Be flexible.

4
Generic Midwestern Directional University

With Decibel ending up in the Big Apple, we also got schooled in the subject of housing costs for students. Her rent soared to skyscraper heights—although, the fact that rent can be an enormous expenditure when sending a kid to college was not a lesson with which we were wholly unfamiliar. Housing The Piglet in our nation's capital had nearly matched her tuition penny for penny.

At least with The Boy our nest egg wouldn't take quite the beating that it had with the girls. Unlike his sisters, who attended highly regarded private institutions in big cities, he was heading to one of those state universities with a direction in their name, in a generic little Midwestern college town. A Southwest Central Northern State U type of thing. Generic Midwestern Directional University (GMDU)—Go Fighting Soybean Shuckers, Go! He had a good reason though; GMDU has an excellent aviation program, his chosen field.

We expected that The Boy's living expenses should be quite a bit lower than we were used to, but still, dorms are expensive everywhere, and there was no telling what apartments went for near GMDU.

It certainly wasn't a part of our plan, or lack thereof, to go broke getting our offspring through school. Plus, if we were going to Go Gypsy, our income would take a major hit. We needed an idea to keep some cash flowing, a brainstorm that would rain down some dough. Banking on Veronica finding freelance tech work while I picked up a gig here and there along the way wasn't going to cut it. I did have an ace in the hole. I had kept a very good relationship with my agent in Europe and continued to tour over there once or twice a year, but that wasn't going to cover us.

Then a thunderbolt struck.

We had always done well with the real estate we owned, so I tossed this notion out to Veronica:

"What if we sell this place and use the money to buy some rental property right near The Boy's school? He can live in one apartment and we'll collect rent from the rest. Bingo, lower costs for college plus some income for us. The old two birds with one stone trick."

No response, but she was thinking. That gave me time to sell her, and myself, on the idea.

As usual, we turned to the Internet for answers. It turned out that we weren't the first people to think of this. Shocking, I know. It's a fairly common method of furnishing housing for students, and it seems to work out well, as long as they don't go all *Animal House* on the place.

Searching a little more, we found some properties for sale in the Generic Midwestern Directional University College Town that The Boy was headed for.

"Look at these—there are some really good deals on these big old houses right near the campus that have been turned into apartments."

While I was looking at possibilities, Veronica started crunching some numbers. It was beginning to make sense to her, to both of us. This might be workable.

"But where will we live after we sell our house?" she asked, sticking a pin in the balloon.

Oops, hadn't thought of that. I guess every idea has some minor details that need to be worked out.

"Um, I'm not sure. In one of the apartments while we figure it out?" I half-asked, half-stated. "We're going to have to be flexible, adapt on the fly. You know, the plan is no plans."

Veronica lifted one eyebrow. A tangible option popped into my head.

"The Boy's college orientation is in a couple weeks. How about I go up with him to take a look at some of these buildings?"

"That makes sense," she said. "We need to know more before we can make a decent decision."

* * * * *

With a few emails and phone calls, we'd lined up a realtor, Smiley WideTie & Associates, ready to show the properties we picked out in The Boy's Generic Midwestern Directional College Town. Next thing I knew, I was flying two thousand miles from our island home with nothing more than a college-bound boy and a big idea.

Smiley himself picked me up at my hotel in the company Cadillac. He informed me that the buildings we chose were all in "the Historic District," realtor-speak for what I learned later is more commonly called the Student Ghetto. These once grand old Victorian houses were long past their expiration date. The maintenance on one of these monstrosities would kill any hope of profit. After looking at a half dozen or so I got the picture, and it wasn't pretty. The best of the buildings were dilapidated. Warning lights started flashing in my head. Being a slumlord was not part of our grand design.

"Are there any other options?"

"There are some condos on the other side of campus," Smiley said. "More students are living over there these days."

A glimmer of hope.

"Let's take a look," I said, hopping back into the Caddy.

We drove over to a very nice one bedroom split-level condo where a graduating student was in the process of moving out. This was more like it. Well kept and ready to rent, with a price that was insanely low compared to what we were used to on St. Croix. I called Veronica right then and there.

"I found a place!" I was pretty excited.

"What's the deal?"

"Well, it's a condo . . ."

I explained the problems with the buildings in the Historic Student Ghetto and how, for what one of those old beat-up buildings cost, we could get several condos. They're newer, closer to the school, and, best of all, have on-site maintenance crews. By the time I got off the phone we were both crazy in love with the idea.

Smiley was ready to deal. He just happened to have paperwork in the Caddy. I made an offer and called Veronica again.

"Start packing" were the first words out of my mouth.

5
Sixteen Boxes

"Start packing."

How could two simple words simultaneously elate me and scare the ever-living crap out of me?

Why were we doing this? Why, after all of those years preparing our children to go out into the world successfully, were we dropping out of it? Was this entire idea of ours just a load of denial and self-indulgence? Would this endeavor end with us returning to St. Croix, tails tucked between our legs, begging for our jobs back?

I didn't know.

I didn't want to confront these issues because that meant facing the hard truth; I had lost a huge part of my identity in the process of growing into adulthood, raising kids, and trying to fit the mold that society had carved out for me. I honestly didn't know who I was anymore. Even scarier, I didn't know who David and I were as a couple.

I needed to find out, and it was going to take a wild adventure to do it. We couldn't go about our regular lives with a big, gaping hole that the children used to fill creating a fissure between us. We needed to break away and find The Beanpole and The Valley Girl again. Use our experiences of growing up together and raising a family to find something more. Something new.

I wasn't in denial about my inclination to run away. When I need a change, I change big. I'm a fan of the clean break. I don't like things to be muddled, and I abhor loose ends.

It also hadn't escaped me that by leaving our delightful little island we would be closer to The Spawn. As much as I knew I had to quit with the helicoptering, my hovering heart still knew what it wanted.

So I began to rid myself of everything except a handful of personal items. We would no longer own a stick of furniture, an appliance, or a bit of clothing that we were not planning to wear in the near future (including those skinny jeans that were hanging around as incentive). I set about paring down our entire lives to fit into a few boxes.

Sixteen boxes to be exact. Twenty-six years of marriage and three grown children later, I whittled everything down to sixteen boxes, most of them going to storage. Many of these boxes were tagged to go directly to one or the other of The Spawn once they were more settled. Some of these, containing photo albums or baby clothes, wouldn't be opened for years.

What is it about boxes, Bubble Wrap, and packing tape that drags us down Memory Lane?

* * * * *

I couldn't bear to part with the baby clothes—a sweet little black and white dress that The Piglet and Decibel both wore; a jumper with an appliquéd Scottie dog, handmade by David's mother, that each of her four sons and The Boy had donned on special occasions.

The boxes were taunting me. They seemed to make our upcoming exploits a bit too real.

"You realize a change is ahead?" they said. They knew I had issues with change.

I was no longer a mommy, but a long-distance mother. I no longer woke up in the middle of the night to breastfeed a sweet-breathed newborn, forced myself to stay awake waiting on a boundary-pushing teenager flirting with her curfew, or had to be up at the crack of dawn to shuttle the brood to school. If I was up late—or early—it was merely because I felt like it. Or, if I had to pee.

"Why is this so daunting?" I asked the boxes.

They simply sat there offering no answers. Apparently, boxes only pose questions.

Prior to breeding, I was fearless. I was still a teenager when I hooked up with a musician and took off across the country. I never thought twice. If one of my daughters had even entertained such a brain-dead notion, my screams would have been heard in Reykjavík. Luckily, said musician was David—but seriously, what the hell had I been thinking?

I was madly in love and had the common sense of a lemming and a consequences-be-damned spirit of adventure. I packed my meager belongings into a giant Chrysler Newport dubbed The Sharkmobile and headed east out of California, destination Nashville. We drove through the desert in un-airconditioned splendor with one of my hands cupping the wind out the window, the other holding David's. Our lovesick eyes saw only beauty reflected in that Chrysler's gigantic hood. If The Sharkmobile had been a convertible, and I owned a headscarf, we'd have been stars in a hippie version of a Grace Kelly movie.

Was I running away? Yup. I was only eighteen, but had already been living on my own for two years. I had known for a long time that a clean break from California was necessary if I were to remain sane.

Had there been a movie called *Nasty Divorce*, it would have starred my parents. They were both wonderful people but had no business being married to each other. Honestly, I don't know what was going through their minds. I have no doubt that they tried very hard to make it work, but their unhappiness manifested itself in insurmountably ugly ways. They called it quits after thirteen hurtful years, the year I turned twelve.

What followed, as is often the case, was a series of tragically bad relationship choices. This led to the constant shuttling back and forth of my brother and myself, never-ending school changes, and just plain craziness.

By the time I turned sixteen, I'd had enough. I had to get off the crazy train and find my own place. So I moved out, worked two jobs while finishing high school, and then hit a wall. I had no idea what to do with my life.

The ensuing summer and fall were spent going to parties, staying out late, waking up at noon, and working the dinner shift as a waitress at a restaurant on the boardwalk in Ventura. My roommate, a thirty-something singer in a bar band, and I somehow scrounged up enough money every month to make the rent on a cute little seaside cabin. Soon enough, it became the crash pad for anyone who happened to show up at the late-night-'til-crack-of-dawn bonfires on the beach.

The combination of Roomie's drug and alcohol problems and my immaturity—and inability to object to the goings-on lest I be labeled uncool—led to some pretty crazy situations. Many a morning I woke up to Roomie tiptoeing into my bedroom to ask me if I remembered the name of the guy sleeping in her bed. I'd have to groggily stumble out into the living room to see who was left. From the headcount I could usually decipher who Roomie's Mr. Lucky must have been. I might have been drifting, but I knew this was not the sort of life I wanted to be living.

I was getting pretty adept at learning what *not* to do by example. But I didn't have any examples of what *to* do—wholesome role models were in short supply, and I wasn't exactly seeking them out. The only certainty was that I didn't want to have kids. I was sure I didn't have the tools to raise them properly—I'd just screw them up.

Running away changed that. It took David and me a few days to get to Nashville, a year to be married, and two years for me to get pregnant. The wild child who was never going to have kids got herself knocked up. And I couldn't have been more elated.

A protective, procreating new me was born; nesty, earth-motherly—and fearful. I worried about everything. What if I ate something that was poisonous to the baby? What if I chose the wrong birthing process? What if I couldn't lactate? The list was endless.

Whilst incubating, I spent hours preparing what passed for a nursery, a sunny little nook off the living room of our rented duplex. I learned three chords on the guitar so I could hold the instrument against my belly and play music (or something akin to music) to the baby. I memorized every parenting book I could get my hands on. I was pigheadedly determined to be the best mother since the Virgin Mary.

The Piglet changed my world. Her little red wrinkly face was the most amazing thing I'd ever laid my eyes on. I couldn't stop looking at her. But mostly I was relieved that my diet of watermelon and instant mashed potatoes, the only foods I could hold down while I carried her, had nourished her just fine.

Two years later, when The Piglet's sister, Decibel, arrived, the What Ifs continued to badger me. Decibel came screaming into the world at full volume, and yet I worried. And when The Boy made his quiet appearance, even with two priors under my belt, I had endless questions.

What if The Piglet never learned to tie her shoes? What if The Boy sneaked out of the house and got into *real trouble*? What if Decibel ran off with a musician? What if that musician was a drummer?

The more I worried, the more I hovered. After all, I was fully aware, firsthand, of all the trouble The Spawn could get into.

* * * * *

The boxes continued to nag me as I made a diagram detailing the location of each item I packed.

"You have no plans!"

It appeared that the boxes were also aware that I was the embodiment of preparedness. Even though our plan as GypsyNesters was *no* plans, the boxes' statement was thought-provoking. Stupid boxes, making me think about stuff.

It is true that I am, deep down to my core, a planner. Years ago I came across a poem my mother wrote that beautifully, and truthfully, described me. It spoke of a child who looked so forward to upcoming events, meticulously preparing for every moment, that when the big day arrived she was always let down. It was high time that kid was sent to her room without supper.

However, I firmly believe this propensity for planning served me well in the parenting department. I made lists, charts, and schematic diagrams to keep track of ballet rehearsals, baseball games, concert practices, and flying lessons. I would scotch-tape the kids' schedule to the glove compartment of our minivan, which we unlovingly referred to as The Whore of Babylon (our affinity for naming vehicles had endured).

She was bright red like a harlot and signified our true entry into the world of Keeping up with the Joneses, which made us feel a little like, well, prostitutes. Constantly in the shop, she screwed us out of money at every turn. David hated her in an epic, almost biblical kind of way.

I would tool around in The Whore checking seatbelts, handing out snacks, asking about schoolwork, keeping Decibel's feet off of The Piglet's "side"—oh, and driving. I must have put a million miles on her as I planned and planned and planned.

But the time has come, dear boxes, for the obsessive planning to end. The plan is for you to be in storage—no matter how much you whine, plead, or intimidate.

"What about our precious cargo?" they asked as I Bubble-Wrapped the living crap out of an heirloom teacup. "Don't you care about *anything* anymore?"

This answer was easy. The stuff in the boxes had been gathering dust on shelves or buried in drawers for quite some time. Not exactly daily-use-type stuff. This was the history of us, my husband and our children, our parents and grandparents, mementos of lives lived. No one in our family was at a point where Memory Lane was a street in their city, much less their neighborhood. And David and I certainly weren't going to live there.

I'll revisit Memory Lane when I'm really old, surrounded once again by these mocking boxes, a crotchety old lady with too many stories to tell, willing to unleash them onto anyone who will listen.

I also know, beyond a shadow of a doubt, that the photo albums, Grandma's china, and the books that I treasured as a child remain precious. Someday, perhaps one of my daughters, a grandson, or a curious anthropologist will cherish my keepsakes too.

But for now, you sixteen boxes, it's time for you to shut up and keep my memories safe in the dark, cool recesses of a storage building.

6
Empty Nest Egg

When The Boy and I returned from Generic Midwestern Directional University, it hit me that Veronica and I only had a couple of months to pull off this Going Gypsy business. The biggest trick would be in the timing. All we had to do was quit our jobs, sell our current place, close on it, move out, send all of our stuff north on a boat, and then get there before it was delivered. What could possibly go wrong?

Veronica had already jumped in with both feet on the packing front. Good thing too, because from prior experience we learned that for me packing means endless hours of debate as I decide the ultimate fate of each letter, knickknack, photo, postcard, thank-you note, shoestring, paper scrap, LP, forty-five, cassette tape, or eight-track that I had saved for no apparent reason.

Within a couple of days we'd given notice at our jobs. Veronica's employment had a built-in ending point, the close of the school year, but she had agreed to stay on a few weeks longer to get things in order, help with the transition, and show the new guy the ropes.

My work situation was even easier to disentangle. Other than my periodic tours overseas, I performed at various beach bars and night spots around the island. Just me and my guitar. At first it had been a welcome respite from Nashville's corporate music business and the soap opera entanglements that come with being in a band. But after eight years, I was ready to disengage even more.

I also did the afternoon slot on a local radio station. It was fun. I got paid to play music that I liked and babble on the air about songs and artists. But it was always kind of a lark for me, something I knew was temporary.

So I told the station manager about our gypsy scheme, played a few farewell shows at some of my favorite haunts, and that was that. We were both officially unemployed.

In the meantime, one phone call and a quick meeting had our house on the market. We were all in. No turning back. Our future had uncertainties galore, but one thing was certain: our offspring would not be returning to live in their old bedrooms.

Good, we thought. We had learned about the phenomenon of adult children returning to the nest from The Piglet on her final visit home before earning her university degree.

We got to talking about her plans. She had some options, chief among them a job offer in DC, where she had been going to college, or taking a big chance and moving to New York to go for it in the concrete jungle.

"Do you know anyone in New York other than your sister?" Veronica was worried about The Piglet making a go of it in the Big Bad Dangerous Apple. "Are any of your friends moving there too?"

"I know a couple of people from my internship, but a lot of people in my class are moving back in with their parents after graduation." There wasn't even a tiny hint of jealousy in her reply. Simply put, she was appalled. "I can't believe they're not dying to get out and start their own lives."

This was our introduction to the idea of Boomerang Kids. The concept was completely foreign to us. Why would any young adult want to do this? The Piglet supplied the answer in her best snooty, sarcastic voice.

"They don't feel like they can afford to live in the style to which they have become accustomed."

I could hardly believe my ears.

"They're not supposed to!"

Where did prior generations live when they were first starting out on their own? Generally not the Taj Mahal. Veronica and I started out in a one bedroom converted screened-in porch that had all the weatherproofing of the average wiffle ball. It was a veritable private zoo of urban vermin, and we were thrilled to have it. We were proud and happy to be self-sufficient.

Accidentally smacking my head on the five-foot-high kitchen ceiling/stairwell overhang a few hundred times made me really appreciate our eventual move up to bigger digs. We rejoiced in every improvement of our living conditions through the years *because* we had worked for it. We moved into a real apartment, then a duplex, until we finally saved up enough to make the down payment for an assumed loan on an about-to-be-repossessed starter home.

The place was a cat pee–saturated disaster, but we worked like crazy on that funky little domicile until it was quite livable, and we tasted the pride of ownership along the way. Who were we to deny our offspring those same pleasures?

There was also a huge financial upside to this process. During the eleven years we occupied our starter home, we established credit, refinanced it to a conventional loan at a much lower rate, built up thousands of dollars in equity, and sold it at a substantial profit. We had stashed away a tidy little sum of money without even thinking about it. None of this would have been possible had we spent our twenties and thirties living with mommy and daddy.

Once The Piglet pointed it out, we noticed the boomerang effect all around us. I sometimes wonder who is more responsible for this sort of behavior—the kids or the parents. For the adult offspring, a free room in the old childhood house, home-cooked meals, no bills, their old familiar bed, and hanging out in the old high school stomping grounds might seem too good to pass up.

As for the parents, I can only surmise that a good number of folks who have Boomerang Kids actually want them to stay at home. Consciously or unconsciously, I think they are unable, or afraid, to give up their role as parents. They are as unwilling to move on to the next phase of their lives as their offspring are. Most tell themselves that they are helping their kids. But does making things easier really help? Does enabling these fledgling adults to hang around the nest and encouraging them to postpone real life do them any good? I think not.

So we wouldn't be taking any chances when it came to The Spawn boomeranging. No Australian hunting stick would be knocking us on the noggin. There would be no nest to bounce back to.

Ever since that funky first place, we faithfully poured money into our homes until our soon-to-be-empty nest had become a tidy nest egg. Why not sell it and use the profit to reinvest and live a little?

* * * * *

Back up in the great Midwest, Smiley WideTie had worked it out so that we could close on our new college town condo long-distance. Utilizing FedEx, fax machines, phones, email, and the occasional carrier pigeon, we managed to buy a property without ever getting within two thousand miles of the previous owner. Ain't technology grand? So, Step One complete. At least we had a place to send our boxes.

Seeing that we were serious about this idea of ours, Mr. WideTie was ready to loosen his neckwear and find us some deals. He called every few days with news about other available properties in the same condominium complex. Having all of the properties in the same place was important to us. That way we would only have to deal with one management and maintenance company.

I told Smiley that we would take a look as soon as we got back up there. What I didn't say was that there wasn't going to be any more buying going on unless we sold our island home.

We were starting to stress out a mite. Should we lower the price? Try to rent it out? Our jobs were ending soon, The Boy had to get to GMDU, and I had booked a late summer concert tour in Italy as a jump start to our gypsy lifestyle. Worst-case scenarios were beginning to run through my mind.

I couldn't book the airline tickets for the tour. Where would we fly out of? Where would we fly back to? What if we were in Europe when the house sold? Well, we already knew how to close a sale long-distance, but from Italy? I thought about the house sitting empty through the upcoming hurricane season with no one there to batten down the hatches, and coming back to a pile of rubble. Doubt was nipping at the edges of my mind.

Then a ray of hope came shining through. Our St. Croix realtor called to let us know that a couple was flying down from the States specifically to look at our house. We cleaned like maniacs and made plans to be out of the way for the Saturday showing.

Sure enough, they made an offer, a good offer, and we took it. They wanted to move in right away, so all of a sudden we had a new problem. We had no place to live for the next few weeks while Veronica finished out her stint at the school. All in all, it was a much better problem to have.

The next week, as we were moving into a one-month rental, The Boy and I carted sixteen seventy-pound boxes to the post office. Seventy pounds was not just some random choice, as if I thought, *Gee, I can lift seventy pounds without needing immediate emergency back surgery, so let's stop there.* It's the maximum that the post office will allow. Here's something we learned: there's nothing a postal worker likes more than a large assemblage of boxes, right at that maximum allowable weight limit, showing up about a half hour before closing time. After this, I doubt we could even mail a postcard from the St. Croix Post Office without them going postal on us. Good thing we were leaving.

* * * * *

With two weeks to spare before The Boy's first day of school, we temporarily plopped down in his Generic Midwestern College Town. We didn't beat the boxes though. They were waiting for us at the post office, with a whole new crew of postal workers ready to go postal.

Within a few days Smiley had shown us several condos, and we snagged a couple that were priced right and ready to rent. With the fall semester just days away, we had student tenants in them both in no time flat. Suddenly we were landlords. One more acquisition and our real estate empire would be complete.

"Why is this one so cheap?" I asked, looking through the latest WideTie & Associates listings.

"I'm not sure. I haven't seen it yet, but it probably needs a little work. Let's take a look at it."

"A little work" turned out to be the understatement of the century. We walked in and found a thin film of an unidentified orange substance coating the entire ground floor. What was this stuff? It thickened as we approached the kitchen. The source must have been in there somewhere.

"It's grease!" Veronica cried out, fighting back the urge to blow chunks all over the mind-numbingly disgusting, grease-soaked carpet on the kitchen floor.

"Oh my God, they carpeted the kitchen?" I added, not helping.

The grease was literally squishing up in little bubbles around our feet as we stepped gingerly on the rug. The source was on the stove, but not a part of the stove. It appeared that the stove had not been functional for some time. In fact, the source looked to be the only functioning appliance in the entire place, a FryDaddy Deep Fryer. Well, if you can't stand the grease, get out of the kitchen. Heeding that paraphrase of an age-old adage, we slogged our way over to the stairs to check out the second floor.

Smiley was not so smiley right about now. He stayed in the front room looking thoroughly disgusted, trying desperately not to come into contact with anything. His tie was perfect.

"How's it look up there?" he called after us.

"At least the walls aren't coated with the orange greasy film," I proclaimed.

Veronica gave my arm a tug and pointed, "The carpet is horrible in this bedroom, and they've torn it clear out of the other one."

"Saves us the trouble," I replied. "Let's check the bathroom."

"Unbelievable," we said in perfect unison.

It was the only word that would enter any normal human's brain at the sight. No need to inspect it further. It was a total loss. We shut the door and retreated back downstairs.

Veronica bounced up to Smiley with, "We love it!"

I threw in, "A bargain at any price."

Our jocularity and sarcasm seemed to puzzle him a bit, as Mr. Wide-Tie was still clearly disturbed by the overall gross factor of the place. He remained all business. So when we offered under three-quarters of the asking price, we made sure it was clear that we weren't kidding. Straight faces all around.

Once he cracked his namesake smile, Veronica nudged me and whispered, "His socks match his tie."

7
Fear Conquering and Writing a Will

I have to admit that some of the humor in our escapades was a defense mechanism. Obviously, in the union of David and myself, I am by far the less fearless. For me, selling the nest and heading out into the big wide world was stepping way outside of my comfort zone. The whopper of a panic attack I had right before we left St. Croix gave a strong indication of my state of mind.

The overload of tying up the loose ends at work, long-distance real estate transactions, last-minute college-mom duties, and emotional farewell dinners with our friends tripped my circuit breakers. I had gotten the boxes to shut up, but wasn't capable of quieting my brain.

Actually, I give myself snaps for spending only one night pacing the floor and panicking. This was a big step toward overcoming my risk aversion. I hadn't taken a big risk in years—unless switching from a Blackberry to an iPhone counts.

For our new life-changing decision, I decided that before I could be comfortable taking on the world, I had one more huge task to complete. No further craziness would happen until our affairs were in order in the event of our certain demise.

It was essential for me to be convinced that The Spawn would not be burdened if I went down in a hang-gliding/bungee-jumping/snowboarding/street-food–eating blaze of glory. They would have enough on their plates explaining to their friends how mommy was gored by a long-horned steer in rodeo clown school. They didn't need probate problems to boot.

We got ourselves to a lawyer to write a will.

* * * *

J. Biffington Goodmannerlyness, Esq., has a somber job and he is very good at it. J. Biff's gig is like a prequel to the funeral director's. Weighty, uncomfortable subjects are handled in a most serious and solemn way. He is calm and crisply coiffed but, unlike a funeral director, doesn't smell of formaldehyde. He smells like soap. Squeaky-clean soap.

We shook hands, exchanged pleasantries, and settled in to a distinguished wood-paneled conference room. His Bifflyness had no clue that he was about to embark on the most inappropriate client meeting of his young career.

I'm not going to lie. Talking about my death—and what happens to the people I leave behind—is not my favorite topic, and when David sees that I am uncomfortable with anything, he morphs into a tasteless nightclub comedian. Right off the bat, he opened with, "So, Biff, let's talk about us becoming stiffs."

Poor J. Biff didn't know what hit him. To his credit, he held fast to a calm demeanor and a strained smile. The Biffinator did his utmost to keep us focused on the task at hand. The more he tried, the more we felt like we had to crack him. He was so adorably serious.

"So, how does this work?" David asked. "I mean, let's say I take the big dirt nap the day after we sign it. What happens?"

J. Biff calmly explained the process. His knowledge and expertise clearly garnered huge advantages over the do-it-yourself–type will. We could ask stupid questions and have a mediator for the inevitable heavy discussions and a sounding board for the intricacies of our family dynamic.

We discussed the sixteen boxes we had in storage. I'd written things like "Grandma's china for Decibel" and "For The Boy on his twenty-first birthday" on the corresponding cartons. A few unmarked knickknacks, pieces of art, and photo albums would be left for them to fight over. What good is a funeral without a scuffle or two? It'll keep their minds off of my corpse—I am a very considerate mother, after all.

I breezed through the bequeathing unfazed. That was the easy part, and that way my mortality stayed off in the abstract. Then J. Biffy brought up the living will. Ugh.

Having personally gone through the pull-the-plug process twice—once with a living will and once without—I am a *huge* proponent of the advance directive method. Making life-or-death medical decisions under duress is not a burden I want to dump on my offspring.

David, when asked about life support, without hesitation said, "First time I poop my pants, throw me off the back of the boat."

He's scary serious about this.

"I'm fairly sure if I offed you for soiling yourself, I'd be facing murder charges." I turned to Biff. "You're a lawyer, help me out here."

"She could face a significant amount of jail time." Did I detect a hint of sarcasm? Uh-oh. The Biffmeister could be onto us. David settled for the safer "no drastic measures" option.

Personally, I was more willing to give adult diapers a shot, so J. Biff gently ran me through some end-of-life scenarios.

Funeral directions were a bit tougher. This really brought home the ultimate demise. I knew I didn't want a grave that people would feel obligated to visit. Whatever part of me that makes me *me* won't be there. Why visit a tiny plot of ground and bones?

The disposal of my dead body gets tricky for me. In some ways I feel like it's not any of my business what happens to it. Those choices should be left for the living. If they need a service and a burial for closure purposes, then who am I to deny them? But I've tried to talk to The Spawn about how they would prefer to deal with these inevitable issues, and they will have none of that. They take after me in that regard.

I've looked online at some options, and there are a surprising amount of them. Burial at sea appeals to me, but entails obtaining permits and hiring a boat with a captain willing to take on the task. I don't want The Spawn stuck holding back puking, seasick relatives' hair as they are trying to grieve.

Being ashes in an urn on a mantle might be a fun way to spend eternity. I could be passed down from generation to generation. Get used as a centerpiece for holidays. Sounds like a lot of fun until some great-great-grandchild drops me and I end up in a vacuum cleaner bag.

I even found a company that will pour me into a cement ball and make me part of a coral reef. Talk about sleeping with the fishes.

Once again David broke in with the wildly inappropriate.

"I want to be stuffed and propped up in a recliner. Stick a cold beer in one hand and the remote in the other. Nobody'll even notice. Dad fell asleep in his chair again. So, Biff, what are the legalities involved with that?"

Gotta love my man.

Sir Biffalot looked like he could use that cold beer right about then. He straightened his paperwork and looked at us seriously. "Clearly you aren't ready for final arrangements. This is something you two need to discuss with your family and get back to me on."

We signed some documents and Biff told us he'd have the final will ready for us in a few days. That wasn't so bad.

The best part was knowing that The Spawn will have sweet, compassionate J. Biffington Goodmannerlyness at the ready when the time comes. He'll know just how to act when they start wisecracking away their grief.

We've already broken him in.

8
Sardinia Has the Best Donkey

While Veronica had her bouts of panic, the sheer pace of events over the summer held my anxieties at bay. There simply wasn't time to worry too much about any decision. Sell it, move it, buy it, and rent it, so far, so good. I projected complete confidence throughout the process, but that was mostly for Veronica's sake. In reality, the doubts that I had were overshadowed by more immediate concerns.

With the bulk of those chores and doubts behind us, only the renovation of the grease-coated mess of a condo that we were demented enough to buy blocked our path. But that would have to wait.

On The Boy's first day of college, we were getting on a plane. Generic Midwestern College Town–Chicago–New York–Zurich and finally Sardinia. We didn't really plan for the two events to happen simultaneously; it just worked out that way. As luck would have it, my short tour in Italy coincided exactly with our officially empty nest.

I've always considered the travel and opportunity to see new places a huge plus to my occupation as a musician. It may not have made up for all of the time spent away from my family, but at least it was a bright side. In the nineties, I had the good fortune of making connections in Europe that led to more than twenty tours with half a dozen or more artists. The majority of that time was spent in Italy, and Italia became my home away from home. My agent was in Cuneo, my record company in Milan, and I had friends scattered throughout the country.

Fortunately, I kept in touch, so I still get to fly over and perform every now and then. Even better, unlike back when the nest was filled and the brood needed tending, Veronica could join me and make it a working vacation, as well as a kick-ass kickoff to our empty nest.

When I met Veronica she was terrified of flying, so much so that she nearly drew blood while squeezing my arm on our rough honeymoon flight. As the years passed, she got better. Still, I always take her hand before takeoff. If we go down, we're going down together.

"We did it," I said, giving her hand a squeeze as the plane pulled onto the Generic Midwestern runway.

It was what we were both thinking.

"I know," Veronica said, and then added something totally out of character. "If we die now, it won't really matter."

"Huh?"

"I mean if the plane crashes, the kids will be okay. We're done. They can all fend for themselves now."

Wow. No lamenting at all—she was really letting go.

"Well, I hope they won't be celebrating our demise, but you're right, we really have done it."

Our primary job as parents was complete.

* * * * *

The first Sardinian concert was in the town of Sassari. It was more of a city than a town, really. With about a quarter of a million people, it's the second largest on the Mediterranean island.

At dinner before the show, our host, concert promoter, and veritable treasure trove of Sardinian lore, Gianluca, gave us the lowdown on local history and customs. We got a good laugh when the waiter translated a pork dish as "the beef of the pig," and that turned the conversation to food, meat in particular. Gianluca, perhaps looking for a reaction, brought up that horse and donkey are the regional specialties of Sardinia.

"This can be hard to eat for people not from our island," he said with a wry smile.

Was that a challenge? Had the gauntlet been thrown down? How could we face Gianluca over the next few days if we did not eat his "regional specialty"? Since, on a previous visit to Italy, I had been so hungry I could have eaten a . . . um, had consumed horse, that left us with ass. We must eat the ass.

The next day, in a tiny piazza near our hotel, we happened upon an intriguing little café called Trattoria da Peppina. Perusing the signboard out front, we spied asinello, Italian for little donkey. Upon further inspection, baby burro was one of the least adventurous menu items. Spinal cord, small heads of lamb, various entrails and organs, three kinds of snails, and goat feet were all available for our luncheon enjoyment. There were also several offerings we couldn't decipher, even with our fairly complete English–Italian dictionary. That must have been the *really* good stuff.

We had no doubt that this was it, we had found our place. Since we were early—it was barely noon—we had the place to ourselves. The bartender/waiter/dishwasher/cook came out to take our order with a "Prego?"

I replied with what I assumed was a perfectly normal order for this place, "Si, due pasta Bolognese, e un asinello per favore."

Veronica was chowing down breadsticks.

"Are you trying to fill up so you won't have room for ass?"

"No, no, I'm just hungry. I can hardly wait for the ass."

"Yeah, right." Then I mentioned hopefully, "It would be good if there's a nice sauce to cover our ass, or even better, maybe they'll batter it up and throw it in a deep fryer, you know, chicken-fried ass."

While we were enjoying our pasta prima piatti, the distinct sound of naked meat sizzling on the grill drifted in from the kitchen.

Sure enough the ass was served straight up, grilled to perfection, all alone on the plate except for a lemon wedge. Perhaps by accident, but perhaps not, it had a shape that could easily have been seen as a toilet seat.

"That's some nice-looking ass."

"There's nothing like a good piece of ass."

"How'd you like to bite my . . ." Okay, okay, enough of that.

We added the lemon and some salt while we summoned up our courage. I cut the steak, rather tentatively, and gave it the sniff test. Smelled good, looked okay.

"Here we go. The fork is up and . . . it's good!"

No, really, it was good. Fully expecting to only try a bite or two, we ate every bit. It was genuinely tasty, and best of all, at dinner that night we could truthfully say to Gianluca, "No grazie, we had ass for lunch."

* * * * *

After a few days and a couple of shows in Sardinia, we made our way back to the mainland for dates in Torino, Ovada, Genoa, Alba, and Casale Monferrato, with some time off in between for sightseeing. Even though none of these towns is at the top of the tourist's must-visit list, they all have fascinating stories and architectural treasures.

Genoa is a whole lot more than the home of delicious dry salami. It is the Unofficial Capital of the Italian Riviera, the stretch along the Ligurian Sea between Pisa and the French border, and easily one of Italy's most enchanting cities. It is also the birthplace of Christopher Columbus, as well as the only slightly less world-renowned guitar picker and collaborator on the tour, Paolo Bonfanti.

Upon learning of our arrival, Paolo's mother, Mama Bonfa, insisted that we make a pilgrimage to the homestead. She prepared a feast fit for royalty and welcomed us like family.

This was not to be a typical Italian meal, but more of a traditional Ligurian repast. Genoa is known as the home of pesto, which was invented here, so guess what we were having? Mama Bonfa was not about to let us leave Genoa without having her handmade gnocchi with the classic basil and garlic pesto.

While that was the centerpiece of the meal, Mama Bonfa circulated in and out of the kitchen with focaccia, cheeses, vegetable pastry, salad, and various vinos to round out the sumptuous spread. Every dish was fantastic, and none were a mystery, until late in the meal when Mama emerged from the kitchen with a bowl of odd-looking white stuff.

Veronica quietly asked me what it was. I had no idea. Paolo, musician and translator extraordinaire, must have overheard because he answered, "Gianchetti."

"What?" I had never heard of it.

"Baby anchovies. It is a specialty of the region," he explained.

One of the many advantages of dining in an Italian home, above and beyond the sheer volume of food and never-ending courses, was the opportunity to try dishes not available, or that we would never order, in a restaurant. Gianchetti is certainly one of those. I can't recall ever thinking *I wish we could find some tiny blanched baby anchovies*.

But itty-bitty whole parboiled freshly foaled fishes in a big bowl was exactly what we were having. They looked like oversized grains of rice, or dare I say, maggots, with little black dots that on closer inspection turned out to be . . . *eyes!* There were thousands of little poached eyes staring up at us! Maybe this was a joke. Paolo must be playing *let's see what we can get the Americani to eat.*

But as Mama Bonfa spooned the hatchlings out for all of the Italians present, they seemed thrilled to see the special dish and were digging right in. It must be okay. We were also certain that Mama Bonfa was much too gracious to go along with such a ruse, so we banished that thought.

Common courtesy dictated that we happily accept nice big portions. A little lemon, salt, and olive oil and it was not bad actually, just odd, and a little squishy. Of course when soaked in extra virgin, pretty much anything tastes good.

I leaned into Veronica and whispered, "Not quite as good as ass, is it?"

She was too busy to answer, moving them around her plate, pushing several of the infant fish under some lettuce, accidentally dropping a few into her napkin, and sneakily slipping some onto my plate. She must have done a good job because Mama Bonfa saw her plate and with a broad smile asked, "You like?"

Trapped! What could Veronica possibly say? She managed only unintelligible garble and nodding motions as a gleeful Mama Bonfa piled on a second round, twice as big this time. I might have burst out laughing if not for knowing full well that the vast majority of those little fry were going to end up in front of me. Pass the olive oil, please.

Afterward, I couldn't help wondering why they didn't just wait to let the poor little critters grow up, because a full-grown anchovy can rock a pizza pie.

* * * * *

There's no telling what might be encountered in an Italian hotel. In my travels, I've found that sometimes the accommodations themselves can become an adventure. Through the years, I've seen wild variations in light switches, beds, phones, doors, locks on said doors, and especially bathroom layouts. Much more than just a bidet or no bidet situation, I'm talking complete bathroom philosophies. Like the toilet actually being in the shower, or no definition of a shower whatsoever. It's not uncommon for there to simply be a showerhead sticking out of the wall in the middle of the bathroom and a drain on the floor. The entire room *is* the shower stall, making it imperative to protect vital tissues accordingly.

I've seen bathrooms with a shower curtain down the middle, triangular shower stalls in the corner, groovy circular enclosures (with doors that rarely work without major stickage), and even a shower in the middle of the room. I don't mean the bathroom. A big square glass shower, right in the middle of the main room. The hotel was so proud of it, they had even placed it up on a pedestal and added a light show. It must have been chic because it was at a four-star hotel, but it was not my idea of ideal when rooming with one of the boys in the band.

So as Veronica and I ventured across Italy, I wasn't surprised by any hotel eccentricities we encountered. The same may not be said for Veronica.

* * * * *

I, unlike David, had never spent time all alone in a foreign country, so I was excited at the prospect of roaming the streets of Casale Monferrato solo. This charming little town in northern Italy had me ready to rock. Romantically picturing myself strolling the streets among the afternoon shoppers, I asked David to put together a list of items for a late-night hotel picnic after his rehearsal. He suggested salami, cheese, olives, bread, and wine. I was so excited I practically chased him out of the room so I could get on my way. I gave him a kiss and a shove as I kicked the door shut behind him.

Alone in the hotel room, I hastily changed into what I deemed proper shopping attire, making sure I had my euros, the hotel room key, and David's list. I jotted down the words I needed to know from our handy dictionary—salume, formaggio, pane, vino—and turned to the door. Feeling all Audrey-Hepburn-in-*Roman-Holiday*, I tossed my hair over my shoulder and grabbed the knob. It didn't turn. It was locked.

I stepped back and took a look at the door. Pretty standard set-up—a brass knob with a push-button lock, a deadbolt with the standard thumbturn mechanism. The knob lock's push button was popped out, but the thumbturn was set in the horizontal position. How did that happen? David knew I was going out, and he wouldn't have thrown the deadbolt to lock me in. Maybe it's automatic, a security thing.

I threw the thumbturn to vertical, grabbed the knob and pulled. No good. The knob itself wasn't turning, making me think that the deadbolt was the only thing holding the door shut. But I could hear the deadbolt sliding as I moved it back and forth while I tugged on the door.

An uncomfortable sweat was beading in my hairline. I pushed in the knob button and it popped right back out, which triggered a crazed yanking frenzy and a full-blown sweat.

Then it hit me—call the front desk! Wait. The clerk and I had no language in common; how was I going to explain my predicament? That problem solved itself—there was no phone in the room.

Cell phone! I dug it out of my bag, only to realize I didn't have the front desk number. I frantically rummaged through drawers for an Italian version of the yellow pages, or a matchbook, or anything with the hotel number on it, but came up empty.

Determined not to call David, admit defeat, and catch the on-slaught of teasing that was sure to follow, I sat on the bed and glared at the door. On the other side I could hear someone in the hallway, but my desperation level hadn't reached pound-on-the-door-to-beg-some-weary-traveler-for-help status yet. It's just a freaking door—how hard could this be?

I checked the door hinges to be certain I'd been pulling in the proper direction. I repeatedly flipped the deadbolt while tugging. The stupid thing had to be broken.

Audrey-Hepburn-in-*Roman-Holiday* had now officially become Audrey-Hepburn-in-*Wait-Until-Dark*. Casting all dignity aside, I threw myself at the door and start wailing on it in hope of a rescue. No one around. Crap.

Italian door: 2. Veronica: 0. I admitted defeat.

Reluctantly, I picked up my cell phone and called David.

"Yeah, honey, what's up?"

"I can't get out of the hotel room and don't you dare make fun of me because I'm really pissed off," I said through clenched teeth. "The friggin' lock is broken."

"It's not broken, the button on the knob opens it. You just have to push it . . ."

"*I did that! It won't stay in!*" I yelled, grabbing the unturnable knob.

". . . and hold it in while you pull the door open."

I pushed the button, yanked the handle in a total hissy fit and was knocked to the floor by the force of the flying door.

"Thanks," I sheepishly whispered into the phone. Then I rubbed my thoroughly embarrassed backside.

* * * * *

When I got back to Veronica at the hotel, I didn't rub it in. I really didn't—at least I don't think I did—but she was feeling pretty sheepish, so any mention of doors or locks sounded like a slight to her. I know that I'm usually absolutely terrible about getting a few digs in when there's an opening, so maybe "rub it in" was a relative term.

Anyway, retribution was swift and highly charged. The laptop needed charging. We bought a groovy little multicountry electric plug adapter set right before this trip. It's pretty cool; a US-style outlet attaches to several foreign varieties by sliding onto some electronic connectors and snapping into place.

It doesn't change the voltage, just allows our plugs to fit into European outlets, so we were still dealing with 220 volts. Not a problem. Our computers, in fact most all laptops, can happily charge on 220v current. This was especially useful because we could also charge our phone through the USB port on the laptop.

Once I put my guitar away and stopped teasing her, Veronica asked if I could set up the adapter while she set out our picnic. It was time for justice to be carried out. I'm lucky I wasn't carried out, on a stretcher, through the door that Veronica now knew how to open.

For absolutely no apparent reason, I decided to plug the Italian plug part of the adapter into the wall socket *before* attaching the American outlet part. Then, upon attempting to slide the outlet part on, I bridged the electric connectors with my finger. *Bam*, 220 volts went right through me! I was literally knocked clear across the room.

I caught a break when I didn't soil myself, since our last will and testament now dictated that I be permanently disposed of in that event. I wasn't sure exactly what happened next—because my arms were straight up in the air and my heart was pounding so hard and fast that no other symptoms seemed important—but I think my hair was smoking.

Veronica was laughing. Maybe she waited until she knew I was okay, but by the time I could hear anything over the pounding pulse in my ears, she was laughing.

Payback's a bitch.

* * * * *

By the time our trip wound down, Veronica and I had acclimated to Eurolife to the point where it seemed completely normal. At least we could eat, unlock doors, turn on the lights, flush toilets, open elevators, and plug things in without risking bodily harm.

As a matter of fact, Veronica was starting to fantasize about staying forever, never going back to the States. Maybe she was just trying to avoid the ugly orange mess waiting for us back in Generic Midwestern College Town.

9
Sweat Equity

When Veronica and I returned to good ole US of A, we were hit with a rather large dose of culture shock. In the blink of an eye, we went from Old World refinement, unidentifiable foods, and the perks of life on the road as slightly pampered artists to student housing reconstruction crew.

Perhaps in our time away we had forgotten just how disgusting the oily orange film coating on the apartment was, or maybe it had actually grown. It was quite possibly alive and reproducing.

But a glorious Midwestern autumn was in full swing, my favorite season, and having lived the last decade in the Caribbean, we hadn't seen the four seasons in a while. There are only two in the tropics, hurricane and not hurricane. On the other hand, the onset of fall meant that a serious winter could not be far behind.

Veronica had never experienced a real winter, since she had lived in Southern California, Tennessee, and St. Croix her entire life. She was actually excited at the prospect. She had her heart set on building her first snowman, partaking in a snowball fight, ice skating, making a snow angel, standing on a frozen lake, seeing a hockey game, and maybe even skiing. I, having lived high in the Rockies much of my early life, was well acquainted with subzero weather and therefore slightly less enthused.

But I like to ski, and hockey's okay, so we decided to live in the belly of the grease beast and fight the slime from within while we waited for Old Man Winter to arrive. Conjuring up our best construction worker impersonations, we bought a secondhand bed and moved in.

After finishing the heavy-lifting tasks of floor, carpet, tub, and tile removal, we discovered that paint wouldn't adhere to the walls because of the mysterious vile veneer. We tried every so-called grease-cutting cleanser available within EPA guidelines. The sinister slime simply laughed at them all. After giving serious consideration to using a flame-thrower, we concluded that we must sand the despicable crust off.

It sounded simple enough, until the gelatinous goo gummed up all of our sandpaper in a matter of minutes. The removal of the distressing slime had become the most difficult part of our entire renovation, by far. No matter what we did, as soon as the latest layer of paint dried, traces of the orange became visible. After the fourth coat I began to think it might be a hallucination, but Veronica saw it too, so I trusted my sanity. How many times could we say another coat ought to do it? A few more would be the correct answer.

By the morning of the first snowfall, we had nearly completed our reconstruction. I woke Veronica up and said, "Honey, big news! I don't think that any of the orange grease from hell is showing through anymore, *and* it snowed last night."

There is a magical snow globe–like quality to the world when it's blanketed in the winter's first snow. Veronica couldn't wait to get out in it. The girl had snowman assemblage on the brain since the first big chill blew through back in October, so that was the first thing on the agenda. I remained indoors to make dead sure that the furnace worked up to its full potential.

She had no idea what she was doing, but managed to scrape a pile of frosty precipitation from the grass and fashion it into a snowman. Perhaps snowman isn't the right word; it was more of a snow creature. Veronica didn't care. She loved it, or him, I guess, and took to calling it The Replacement Boy.

When she finally came inside, I told her to stay bundled up because garbage never sleeps. I gathered up a couple of bags of household trash, and Veronica followed me out with a bunch of remodeling refuse. We ventured across the vast expanse of snow-covered parking lot on a trek to the dumpster. Little did we know there was ice beneath that snow.

Suddenly my feet were no longer under me. In fact, they were directly out in front of me, in midair. In a perfect comedy pratfall I went *whomp*, flat on my back. Garbage was strewn everywhere, across the immaculate new-fallen snow. A week's worth of rubbish highlighted nicely against the pure white canvas. A work of art. A Picasso in wilted lettuce, empty wine bottle, and used Kleenex.

"Are you all right?" Veronica was genuinely concerned, only it was hard to tell through her laughter. I couldn't blame her. It really was a classic acrobatic slapstick tumble.

All right? Taking a quick inventory, I found I couldn't move, or talk . . . or breathe. It felt like I was dying. None of this fell under any definition, no matter how broad, of all right. No way to let her know this though, since I could not make a sound.

"Honey, are you okay?" She wasn't laughing anymore.

I couldn't answer. My lungs no longer seemed to work. I remembered this feeling from way back when I was dumb enough to play wide receiver in pickup games and had the life breath belted out of me by some testosterone-crazed teenage cornerback.

I made a Herculean effort to roll over off of my back, hoping it might help me ingest a few oxygen molecules, and caught a glimpse of Veronica. She was headed my way in little-tiny-slippery-shuffle steps, determined not to replay my scene. She failed. Dapples of greasy, orange-flecked construction scraps were added to the masterpiece.

I managed to make it to a slumped-over, hands-and-knees position, allowing a few puffs of frosty air to grace my lungs. Just enough breath that I could show some slight bit of concern for Veronica's well-being. She was okay. She did a much better, but not nearly as uproarious, job of falling than I did.

We attempted to carefully, very carefully, gather and rid ourselves of our garbage before the neighbors could set up their YouTube-enabled video cameras, but, like two dogs in the back of a pickup truck bouncing down an Indiana farm road, all we could do was claw for the slightest hint of traction.

"You wanted to see winter."

10
Fear Conquering and Snow Skiing

Learning to ski at my age had me worrying about things that a younger person might not have. What if I plummeted over a cliff, broke my hip, and died from complications a week later? What if I took a blow to the back of my head from one of those chair ride thingies and ended up like an amnesia-riddled soap opera character? What if I ended up like Sonny Bono and that horrible tree? What if?

I continually needed to remind myself when I started "what if-ing" that the huge majority of "ifs" turn out just fine, sometimes even excellently. Besides, my affairs were in order, my kids grown, and my life burden-proofed. Should I take the big spill, the world would go on without me.

It wasn't just my age and possible frailty that had me concerned. I had a seriously bad track record when it came to delving into winter weather pursuits. I've actually been dragged to an ambulance by the ski patrol, quite a feat since at the time I'd never strapped on a pair of skis.

When the kids were still at home, we hit the slopes a few times with friends, and I was always the adult who volunteered to stay behind with the young 'uns who were too little or disinterested in skiing. It wasn't that I was so magnanimous—I just wasn't big on strapping boards to my feet and sliding, or more likely falling, down a mountain. I wasn't used to snow. During my formative years in the Southern California desert, we preferred to spend our time skateboarding in abandoned swimming pools.

Luckily, most of the ski areas we visited had alternative activities in which non-skiers could partake. In North Carolina, The Boy and I decided to take on tubing—a sport where one clings to a large inner tube while hurtling down a mountainside. Unlike bobsledding or luge, there is no steering, brakes, or control of any kind. It's more like a potato getting flung down an icy chute. At the bottom, the rider is slowed by rounding a steeply banked curve that ends with tube and rider flying up the neighboring chute, where they come to a stop. A sport with no skill involved, just hanging on for dear life. My kind of action.

After a few exhilarating runs together, The Boy, five or six at the time, felt confident enough to slide solo, so we giddily climbed the stairs for another go. In a perfect world, the monitor at the top of the two chutes would be paying close attention to the spacing of the participants, and not flirting with cutely dressed ski—um, *tube* bunnies. But on that particular day, I was not living in a perfect world.

I helped The Boy launch his tube and laughed as he went plunging down the mountain, then readied myself while the attendant helped a giggling tube bunny onto her inner tube in the chute next to me (tube bunnies are such helpless little creatures). Once Bunny's tube came to a stop at the bottom, I was given the signal to head down.

That's when things went terribly awry. Somehow the enormous guy next to me was sent down the mountain prematurely.

As I hit the bottom curve at top speed, Enormous Guy was about three quarters down his chute, careening toward me at even higher speed because of the weight-to-rubber-on-frozen-H_2O-inertia-ratio theory. The last thing I can recall is a massive knee headed right for my cheekbone.

Knocked thirty feet from the impact point, I was out cold. Upon regaining consciousness, I heard:

"Dude, you missed it, that lady got hit in the face *so hard*. Awesome."

* * * * *

Past concussions aside, I really was looking forward to learning to ski. David had put up with quite a bit of my snow-related antics. The man could not go outside without me hitting him on the back of the head with a snowball. I was obsessed with perfecting my technique. Hopefully skiing would be something we could enjoy together.

Exotic words like *packed* and *powder* were being flung about by the giddy skiers surrounding me, and I found it very infectious. So with a smile on my face, on a crisp, sunny day, I was ready to charge the mountain.

At the lodge's rental counter, David helped me into the daunting ski equipment as if he were dressing a two-year-old, complete with runny nose. I was horrifyingly inept. The boots alone were very complicated buggers. They were foot prisons made of a brutal, inflexible, space-age polymer that doesn't exist anywhere in nature. For maximum support, the footwear apparently must be clamped down tight enough to cut off all blood flow below the knees. My legs were getting all tingly, and I couldn't feel my feet at all.

Since that seemed to mean that I was properly booted up, David led the way toward the slopes with our skis and poles. I basically had to relearn the art of walking in order to follow him. Add in two pairs of pants, four layers on top, scarf, hat, and gloves, and my limbs stuck out like a starfish. I did manage to shuffle my way across the room toward the exit and still keep my good humor intact. I was even starting to find it quite comical.

Until I got to the stairs.

My feet might as well have been nailed to the floor. The boots prohibited me from mounting a single step.

I tried pulling one leg up the first step with my sweating, mittened hands. Squatting a tad, I grabbed my thigh above a bent knee and yanked. My shoulder almost sprung from its socket, but the boot remained firmly planted on the floor. Attempting to execute a crablike maneuver, I shuffled sideways whilst doubling myself over the handrail. Great energy expense with no ascension. But, if I am one thing, that thing is resourceful. I found my method. For the remainder of our stay, I ascended the stairs back-end first. It wasn't pretty, but it worked.

My intention was to first take a lesson, thus enabling the Colorado-raised David to get his gazelle-like self straight to the slopes without having the Old Ball and Chain literally be an old ball and chain.

Unfortunately, an instructor wasn't immediately available, so David escorted me to the Bunny Slope.

He listened to my lame jokes disguised as self-deprecation while he bestowed beginner slope gearing-up tactics upon me.

"Keep your skis sideways to the slope."

"Keep your weight on the uphill ski."

"Pop your boot into the binding."

He might as well have been blithering Swiss Alpine gibberish. Time and time again I misdirected my feet and sent my skis flying. Time and time again David retrieved them. The man was a saint.

I tried to keep his pending canonization in mind as he pointed me toward a clanking contraption of spinning frozen rope dragging Gore-Tex coated three-year-olds with boards strapped to their feet up a gentle rise.

"What the hell is *that*?"

He had to be kidding if he thought I was going to attach myself to that thing.

"The rope tow."

More Alpine gibberish. He looked at me as if I were one of the three-year-olds.

"That's how we go up the hill."

Good thing I was very determined to master skiing, because the rope tow was almost as determined to kill me. These gizmos are not made for anybody with a center of gravity higher than Minnie Mouse. It was a thing of beauty—my stiff starfish self being dragged up a slippery surface while flailing forward and back. I looked like one of those dancing inflatable men at a car dealership. Add waving ski poles to the mix and it was gorgeous, a sight to behold.

Standing atop the mountain erroneously called a Bunny Slope, David coached me in the art of snowplowing and edge-digging before pointing me downhill. The boots' tightness and bulkiness disappeared when put to proper use. I miraculously skied that horrifically steep and challenging Slope of the Small Hare without wiping out.

After I'd done the same thing two whole times, Jules, my ski instructor, met us at the foot of the hill. Ready to show off my new moves, I waddled across the flat expanse between us and promptly fell flat at her feet. This did not bode well for my first lesson, the chairlift.

David and Jules discussed my abilities and potential while I flailed deliriously, trying to get back up on my skis. Had they not noticed me down here?

After what seemed like ten mortifying minutes, I was ultimately hoisted upright with assistance from both David and Jules, and I then began my slide toward the chairlift.

Jules and I entered the long queue, and I watched in horror as my fellow skiers nonchalantly hopped on the chairs with dead-on timing. Timing looked crucial because the chairs moved at lightning speed and never stopped. Jules explained to me that for successful execution of the boarding procedure I must be in the proper position.

"Keep your knees bent. Stick out your butt. Skis must be pointed forward. Hold your poles in your outside hand."

I opened my mouth to ask Jules what the poles were for, but after visualizing myself slipping in front of the speeding chair, knocked comatose, lifted up by the scruff of my jacket, carried fifty feet up, and then dropped to my death, I decided instead to concentrate on the task at hand.

I followed Jules's instruction to the letter. With eyes squeezed tight, I felt a slight bang on the back of my legs, and I was up! Must be how a toddler feels when an adult comes from behind and sweeps him off his feet with no warning—both vomit-inducing and exciting.

Because I had been so worried about getting on this crazy contraption, I never considered how beautiful it would be once I was up in the air. The world was peaceful and white, like an old-fashioned Christmas card. Snow-laden trees stood starkly against the bright blue sky. I took it all in and immediately understood why people love winter so much. Then I made a big mistake.

I looked down.

We were just hanging by a thread! Living in a world with mandatory seatbelt laws, I found it very unnerving to be three miles above the unforgiving ground with absolutely nothing to hold me in. To take my mind off the wide-open spaces below, I chatted up Jules.

Next thing I knew, we were about to get off.

"What happens if I can't get off?" I asked Jules.

"What do you mean *can't* get off? You mean if you *decide* not to get off? Not an option." Jules called my bluff. "Just do like I tell you and you'll be fine. Keep your tips up. Here we go!"

Holding my ski poles in one hand as Jules instructed, I tipped my skis up and felt the ground come under them. Emitting a strange squeak, I left the chair and made it down the slight incline in one piece. I came to a stop and turned to flash a triumphant grin at Jules—and fell on my butt. Jeez.

I managed to regain a sitting position, but Jules was determined to have me get up on my own. Problem was, I'd fallen in the path of the skiers and snowboarders exiting the lift behind me. The chairlift stops for nothing. Snow dudes and bunnies whizzed by to my left and right in no perceptible pattern. My biggest fear was that someone of my same skill level was about to fall over me and we'd become a tangled mass of rental gear, goggles, and embarrassment. Jules gave in. She sighed, popped off my skis and dragged me to my feet away from danger.

Grinning wipeouts aside, Jules decided I was ready for Jelly Bean Hill and Candy Cane Lane. Daunting stuff, those. I breezed through like a pro. I'd become Suzy Chapstick with the wind blowing through my honey blond hair—mall bangs and all. No longer was I afraid of the Dr. Seuss–type characters on snowboards zooming by from above. I was on fire. Jelly Bean Hill—I own you!

Having done her job, Jules handed me back into David's capable hands. This time I was unquestionably vertical. David, who had just come from skiing trails with names like Big Cajones and Black Diamond Death Bowl, urged me to try some harder slopes. The really tough ones, like the semi-dreaded Licorice Gum Drop Mountain.

I relented and, after showing off my new chairlift prowess, went to peer over the edge of the slope. Thank God my boots were so tight that my knees couldn't buckle at the sight of the drop-off—that was one mother of a Gum Drop. I refused to budge. David slyly changed his tactics from coddling to out-and-out mocking—until I bit my lip, closed my eyes, and dug in, hoping to snowplow my way down the mountain.

Nope, too steep. Instead I turned and careened straight sideways across the slope. Not having covered this special kind of stupidity in my lessons, I did what came naturally. I freaked out. Ridding myself of the poles, which seemed logical since I still had no clue why I'd been carrying them around all day, I laid out flailing in the snow hoping to stem the velocity of my slide. It did, but not all that well. My full-body sprawl finally skidded me to a stop about twenty feet below my initial impact crater—and my poles.

"You lost your poles, dumbass," was the first thing I heard. "Now I have to climb up there and get them."

"Don't call me dumbass—I'm trying as hard as I can," I pouted.

David insisted that "dumbass" wasn't actually included in the statement. I'm inclined to believe him. We'll just call it *dumbass implied* and leave it there.

Regardless, I was not about to let David come riding to the rescue. I was going to retrieve the poles myself.

Incidentally, it is much less problematic to return to the upright and locked position when collapsed on a steep hill, so I had that going for me. Using my skis' edges, my left hip, and my shredded dignity, I managed to worm my way up to the orphaned poles. I soldiered on to conquer the dastardly Gum Drop. Multiple times.

Now that I'd mastered the kiddie slopes, I felt there might be hope for me on skis. It really *is* fun to zoom around on the white stuff. That is why people do it, right? I don't have to be fabulous to have a great time.

Maybe I'll even stick around long enough next time to find out what the poles are for.

11
windycity420

No broken bones. We were more than a little sore, but all in one piece. No small feat considering I hadn't been on skis in over a decade and Veronica never had. The respite did us good, and we were almost finished with our reconstruction project. There was still one small screw in the works. Once the newly degreased condo was rented out, where would we go? Back to the islands?

It had long been a semi-plan of ours to find a boat and float around the Caribbean after the kids left. We figured we could pick up work along the way and become windblown yachties. Back when we were living in Tennessee, we took a rare kid-free vacation that sprouted the seed of this yacht dream from the fertile ground on the island of Tobago.

That's when we fell in love with the Caribbean. We even tried to buy a small hotel there and escape to the tropics. I could cook and play guitar in the bar while Veronica ran the desk, did the books, and brought in guests from the far corners of the globe with her mad Internet skills. The kids could run barefoot, play in the surf, and meet people from all over the world.

It sounded great, probably a whole lot better than it would have been in real life, but the legal issues of owning a business in a foreign land and the owner's island-time lack of urgency to sell scuttled our big idea. Yet our island fever endured.

Several years later, the fates conspired to push us into treating that malady. Veronica's living room web design company had grown to over one hundred clients. What began as a sort of hobby, back when the Internet was not much more than a novelty, was devouring our domicile. My little Techno Nerd had parlayed what started as an experimental project of making a website for my band into a full-blown business, creating homes on the Internet for some of Nashville's biggest stars. Before long, our living room looked like NASA Mission Control. Houston, we have a problem.

Veronica knew things had outgrown our available space. That, and the fact that she could never get away from work because it was always waiting right outside our bedroom door, meant something had to give. She decided to either move the operation into an office or sell it outright. When an offer came from a larger design company, she didn't hesitate.

Meanwhile I was in the midst of a bad cliché, right in the middle of every quintessential music business legal tribulation imaginable. My latest recording contract had disintegrated into three years of wrangling with lawyers, executives, producers, record companies, ex-managers, agents, publishers, and bandmates. I'd had enough. I went to my manager and told him I was done. The next day we bought tickets for an exploratory visit to St. Croix.

I knew about the island from friends who had worked there, and since it is US territory we could relocate just like moving to a different state.

We flew down to look at houses, explore work prospects, and check out the school possibilities for the kids. Everything seemed very viable, and in fact the school situation looked to have a big upside compared to what we were facing in Nashville. Instead of having three kids attending three different schools, they could all go together and receive what looked to us to be a much better education.

We jumped in and, after an initial adjustment period, took right to life in the Virgin Islands. In hindsight, it was one of the best things we ever did for our family. To this day, all three children consider St. Croix home.

Part of us does too. In our boat dreams, Christiansted Harbor is always our home port. But now that we had the chance to make that dream a reality, something didn't seem quite right. After spending the past decade on an isolated island, we missed our stateside family and friends. Our nearest relatives had been more than a thousand miles away. There were loved ones in Nashville whom we hadn't seen since we left, and Veronica had relatives on the West Coast we had not been able to visit in at least a decade.

We generally only made it up to the States once a year, and after the girls went off to college, that annual trip meant going to see them. Sometimes folks would meet up with us, and other times people came down to visit the island, especially in the winter. But all in all we had been pretty out of touch.

So when we were getting ready to leave the formerly oil slicked abode, reconnecting became priority number one. But how? The logistics were daunting, to say the least. Our relatives and friends were scattered across the country from New York to Los Angeles. That would mean dozens of flights. Where would we stay? We'd need rental cars, restaurants, taxis, trains, and buses. It sounded like an awful lot of planning considering our no-plans plan. Plus, the price tag could easily spill into five figures, scrambling the nest egg.

"What if we got a motor home?"

It just popped into my head, so I blurted it out. I got no answer. Veronica was thinking, possibly that I was crazy. I started working on the idea aloud.

"For what we would spend on airplanes, hotels, and rental cars, we could buy an old RV and then get rid of it when we're done. We could stop and see stuff along the way, you know, hit the hotspots, and we'd have our bed with us every night. Then, if we're lucky, we can sell it for about what we paid for it."

As it turned out, she didn't think I'd completely lost my mind, which was nice. "It sounds like it might work," she said. "Yeah, it just might be the answer."

She looked a touch worried and added, "But this doesn't mean we're never getting a boat, does it?"

"Isn't an RV just a land boat?"

Veronica lifted an eyebrow. I knew that look.

I backpedaled with, "The plan is no plans, right? Let me look into the motor home idea some, see what they cost and stuff. Let's see if it's even feasible."

So I did a little research and learned what to look for in a used RV. Obviously it needed to be mechanically sound, but smelling the inside could be just as important. If it smells musty, there's probably a leak, and leaks are not your friend, unless living with fungus and replacing carpet constantly sound like fun.

In addition to running well and not smelling like a damp basement, there were a couple of other criteria that needed to be met. I needed enough room to stand up inside, and have some buffer space, since I bash my body on things on a regular basis, often drawing blood. I'm so bad about it that one of The Boy's junior high friends once asked Veronica while I was changing a tire, "Isn't it a good thing that Mr. James isn't a hemophiliac?"

I also didn't want some giant land barge that would be impossible to park or maneuver in cities. Ideally, something old enough to have a precomputerized engine that I could change a filter on without needing an engineering degree. It had to have a sleeping loft over the cab, both for space efficiency and because I knew that there was no way we would make up and stow away a fold-down bed every day. We had to have a full bathroom (showering is important) and a decent kitchen, since the avoidance of eating every meal at restaurants was part of the point. Oh yeah, heat and air conditioning would be nice too.

After a little looking around, spending around ten grand seemed reasonable, but dealer selections in that price range were not great. I decided to try eBay. There were quite a few RVs listed, and the bids seemed rather low, well under our ten thousand threshold, but I faced a dilemma with purchasing a vehicle online. There's no freakin' way I was bidding on something I hadn't been able to test-drive. So I limited the search to cities that were reasonably close to good ole Generic Midwestern College Town.

Chicago! Close enough. I called a guy with the eBay handle of windycity420 and explained that we were interested in his motor home, but wanted to test-drive it first. He understood, so we arranged to meet in a few days, a couple of hours before the online auction ended. That way, if we liked the RV, we would be there to put in the final bid right at the last second.

Right before hanging up, windycity420 told me, "Bring cash."

On the final day of the auction, the bid was still under $3,000. I was thinking how great it would be if the thing wasn't a piece of junk and we could get it that cheap. With high hopes and forty C-notes in my pocket, we headed off to Chicago.

The RV was parked in Mr. 420's driveway, so I gave it the old once-over before we knocked on the door. She was an old gal, a 1983 Chevy, but looked well cared for. So far, so good.

Windy opened the door, and we were knocked back by an old familiar aroma. There is no possible scenario in which a person can spend thirty years in the music business and not know that smell. I don't care if it's rock, blues, bluegrass, jazz, opera, classical, country, gospel, or whatever, I guarantee that even the guys who played on *Barney and Friends*'s "I Love You, You Love Me" theme song would know with one whiff what was going on inside Windy's house.

"Dude, Windy's a stoner," Veronica whispered out of the side of her mouth. We hung back, fearing a contact high.

Windy grabbed his hoodie and proceeded to give us the nickel tour of the RV. It smelled of reefer and German shepherd, but no dampness. The inside was in good shape, everything was in working order, and nothing was wrong that a little Febreze and a thorough cleaning couldn't fix. Veronica dubbed it "cute" and covered a giggle with her hand. Had she inhaled too much of the vapors?

Then we fired it up, the motor home that is, and it leapt to life. Always a good sign. As we took it for a spin around the neighborhood, there were some squeaks and rattles, but nothing out of the ordinary considering its age. I was getting kind of buzzed about it—it seemed perfect—but wait, was that the secondhand smoke talking? Well, in any case, I decided then and there that I was going to make a bid.

Then out of the blue Windy says, "I want you guys to have it."

"Huh?"

"Yeah, you remind me of a couple of old hippies. You should have it, man."

Um, okay.

"Well, we like it, but let's see what the bid gets up to."

"Screw the bid, dude, I want you to have it. Give me thirty-two hundred and we'll just put in ten grand as a final bid. No one will out-bid that."

"Uh, yeah. What do you think, honey?"

Veronica was making herself at home, checking in the fridge for munchies. There was no way we weren't buying the thing.

"Let's do it."

So we rolled back to Windy's place. Did a little business. Got offered a toke for the road. Declined. And drove off in twenty-three feet of rolling luxury.

Our first stop was at a store to buy some Lysol. Maybe that would throw the dogs off the scent if we got pulled over.

12
BAMF

The drive back from Windy's place gave us a pretty good idea of what needed to be taken care of with the motor home before we took off on any transcontinental excursions.

David was dealing with the outside stuff—replacing screws, tightening belts, and talking to mechanics. He would slide out from under our new rolling house covered in grease, grime, blood, and the waterproof caulk he was using to seal everything in his path. He was in hog heaven.

I was relieved that he was happy outside, where his bull-in-a-china-shop tendencies would do less harm.

But not for long.

We had ownership of our new toy just one day when the bull charged inside and broke the main overhead light fixture with a broom handle. It wasn't a major deal, nothing that a skillfully placed dab of superglue couldn't fix, and I am a master supergluer. So we agreed that I would run over to the store for some glue while David promised to confine his work to the exterior of the RV. That way I could get the fixture fixed and things more organized indoors before the bull stampeded again. No telling what other broom handle–like destructive implements could be lurking about.

I believe that David's tendency to break things and injure himself is not because he is clumsy. He's not. My theory is that it stems from the way he grew so tall, so fast, as a child. He never quite figured out his proportion to the world around him. According to family lore, when he was in his thirteenth year, he was so skinny that his hands looked like olives on the end of toothpicks. It's a challenge to overcome dimensions like that.

Back from my errand, with a sack of hardware goodies in hand, I opened the RV door to find David standing in the middle of the kitchen area, messing with the overhead light fixture. To add a little spice to the mix, the light was *on*. The man will never learn about electricity.

"I found some superglue."

"I thought we agreed I would fix that."

"But I found some glue, so I figured . . ."

"Well, turn the light off. You're going to electrocute yourself."

"I can't."

"Will you *please* just go outside?" I was trying really hard to keep my cool.

"I can't."

"Dammit! Stop saying you can't and just go outside!"

"I can't."

"Why not?!"

That was when I noticed the shreds of paper towel attached to his free hand and a few tatters clinging around the corners of his mouth. His other hand was space-age-polymer-bonded to the overhead light fixture, which was now permanently secured in the ON position.

* * * * *

The motor home was old and didn't have all the pretty bells and whistles found on newfangled behemoths. No microwave, dishwasher, or coffee machine—those suck down too much power and take up too much space. They could also turn into dangerous missiles when en route. And the oven and refrigerator were dinky; we wouldn't be cooking Thanksgiving dinners for the family in this kitchen.

The bathroom was tiny, but I found the humor in it. If I closed the toilet seat and perched at the perfect angle, I could use the mirror over the sink and have a vanity.

I didn't want to do a lot of remodeling—I'd had quite enough of that lately—but I could not abide the craggy 1970s earth tones and wheat stalk wallpaper. Something had to be done. Not wanting to sink a bunch of money into a vehicle of such advanced age, I gave myself a budget of $150 and got to work on making the place homey.

Deciding to add some flair, I bought two area rugs and a runner in a red-and-rust bold, boxy pattern, a slipcover for the couch in red-on-red vertical stripes, a small can of bright ruby paint, and some gold glitter. As I worked, I daydreamed about how I would have a brand-new view out of the windows every day. No amount of redecorating could hold a candle to that image.

Voilà. In just a few hours the formerly hideous wallpaper in the kitchen and bathroom areas became red and sparkly. The carpet was mostly hidden. The slipcover looked good, even if it was going to need constant tweaking, and considering the couch was basically an elaborate water tank cover, I'd just go with it. Most satisfying, the lingering eau de cannabis and canine were gone.

I excitedly snapped some pictures of my handiwork and shot them off in an email to The Piglet and Decibel. I wasn't expecting a whole lot of enthusiasm, considering The Boy's initial reaction to our gypsy wagon was, "You guys are going to *live* in your *car?*" Kids these days.

I nervously awaited the girls' responses. I certainly didn't want to go through life being an embarrassment to *all three* of my kids. One of them should understand, right?

I immediately heard back from The Piglet, who pronounced my handiwork "cute." Sweet relief poured over me. The Piglet, now a big-city journalist, is quite the style diva. She moonlights on weekends as a hostess in a Soho restaurant just to keep herself in designer shoes. I was over-the-moon at her reaction. The girl obviously has taste.

When Decibel's reply popped up in my inbox it went one step further, "He's BAMF. When do I get to come on a trip?"

BAMF? I had to Google it. Hmmmm—makes sense. Our radiant, fast-walking, subway-chasing, F-bomb-dropping, black-wearing, taxi-flagging, urbanite daughter had named our new vehicle. BAMF. Bad Ass Mo Fo. Brilliant child.

It seemed right, though, and totally in keeping with our vehicle-naming tradition. So it stuck.

* * * * *

BAMF was ready to roll. Part of the fun of mobile living would be learning as we went, or so I was telling myself. Some modern-day conveniences would be easier to give up than others. Even though I had no clue how to heat up leftovers or make popcorn without a microwave, I was fairly certain it was possible. I had to give up my cappuccino machine when we left St. Croix—I had been drinking coffee straight-up since—but now I had to learn to make it on a stove top. A breeze, right?

And what about the days with no Internet access? Or electricity? What would become of my hair without blow dryers, curling irons, and hot rollers? Was I destined for a life of eternal straggly ponytails?

These were just the little things.

As excited as I was to jump into BAMF's navigator seat and roll, there was a nagging, creeping feeling hanging 'round. In the back of my mind's eye, there was a snapshot of David and me stranded on the side of the road surrounded by our meager belongings.

The reality of our new wanderlustful life began to sink in after I pried David's fingers from the light fixture and we spent our first night in BAMF. We had gone about three hundred miles south and found a campground outside of small-town America. We were overjoyed. BAMF had performed brilliantly; we cooked in our little kitchen, and had a few celebratory beers while poking at a campfire. We could do nothing but laugh at our audacity, truly in awe of ourselves for pulling off this whole crazy endeavor. The world was our oyster, and we couldn't decide what to bite off first.

But as we laid ourselves down to sleep in BAMF's loft for the first time, I listened to the crickets, and doubt began to creep in, with a vengeance. Holy crap, The Boy was right—we *were* sleeping in our car.

I sat straight up, a colossally bad idea since the bed loft is only two-and-a-half feet tall, and saw stars when my head collided with the ceiling. The pain sent me over the edge. Let the panic begin! My "what-if" tape loop play button was pressed and the band started rockin'.

What if there are road bandits out there? Could we fend them off? What sort of implements are needed to repel road bandits? Do road bandits still exist?

What if other people think we are *actually* homeless? *Are* we actually homeless? Why do I care what people think? Get real, I care what people think.

What if we get stranded in the middle of the desert? Would we have to wait for days for help? What if we don't have enough water? Does it hurt if a tumbleweed hits you?

What if those aren't crickets I'm hearing? Could they be mountain lions? Do they have mountain lions in Indiana? I'm in Indiana. What would the people of Indiana think of us? Why do I care what . . .

I had worked myself up to the point of tears, but really all of this was secondary or perhaps just a cover for the real question. Could I really do this? Could I really not have a home, a place for Christmas stockings, pictures on the walls, keepsakes that are now all sitting in boxes in a dark storage unit?

Knowing sleep was not going to visit anytime soon, I climbed out of BAMF's loft to get something frozen out of the freezer to soothe my banged-up noggin. Ah, a bag of peas—perfect. My plan was quickly thwarted when I realized that everything in the freezer had defrosted on the trip down. Great, could we *be* more unprepared for our future?

Plopping down on the couch, bag of lukewarm peas balanced on my head, I began an attempt to calmly sort out my fears. Obviously, I had to stop worrying about what people might think of me. Not an easy task, because over the years I had stupidly chosen to value my self-worth by comparing myself to others. Sitting in a beat-up motor home, in the middle of nowhere, with thawing vegetables on one's head and reeking of campfire seemed a scenario that would occupy the bottom rung of any comparison. It might make for a funny vacation story—*remember that time we went camping and all the food spoiled on the first day?*—but this was my new real life. Any hope of embracing it would require that I put my trust in us. Only myself and David, our resurgent Nation of Two, outside opinions be damned.

Acknowledging my public perception problem was a strong step toward recovery, and the only step my brain could possibly tackle that night—the lump on my head saw to that.

Calmer, I returned to the loft, snuggled up with David, and hoped that I would survive the next day, my first Mother's Day without chicks in the nest.

13
Mama Loves a Ball of Paint

Keeping a return of the tears at bay could have been a serious undertaking, but by mid-morning I'd received happy Mother's Day phone calls from all three of The Spawn. Each sent their love and best wishes while expressing their undying gratitude for my bearing them in pain. The waterworks had been held back for the moment, but once the offspring had finished sharing all of the wonderful things going on in their busy lives, the rest of my day loomed menacingly. Weeping was imminent.

This GypsyNesting Mama needed a diversion. It couldn't be just any diversion; it had to be something so spectacular that any sort of baby-missing histrionics would be nipped in the bud. I went over ideas in my head.

A brunch at a really, really nice restaurant? No, just the thought of David and I surrounded by long tables of celebrating families with macaroni-art gifts bestowed by pancake-syrup-sticky hands wouldn't work. The very idea of food reminded me of those wonderful Mother's Day mornings of days gone by. My mind drifted back to the pitter-patter of tiny footie-jammied feet serving up breakfast in bed, featuring shell-fragment-laced scrambled eggs and scraped, smoky toast balanced precariously on a tray with a Kwik Sak–bought carnation sticking out of a soda can for a touch of sophistication. That sort of heaven cannot be duplicated.

After discussing the possibilities, David and I decided that anything even remotely traditional would not do. So what *to* do in the heart of Indiana?

A quick Internet search revealed the attractions in our vicinity. We patiently scanned through several not-as-spectacular-as-needed entries when—eureka!—we hit the mother of all cheesy tourist diversions—the World's Largest Ball of Paint. The best part? It was an interactive display—visitors actually get to paint the thing. Better yet, each coat adds to the ever-growing world record. Just the thought of adding a record-setting layer of pigment to a gigantic paint ball made me forget I ever even had kids.

One snag: the Ball of Paint was viewable by appointment only, so we crossed our fingers and called. Score! The Ball's caretaker would see us on a Sunday (and Mother's Day to boot) with only a few hours' notice. What a guy, he must have felt the pain brewing deep within my heart.

Arriving at the paint ball pavilion, we were struck by the enormity of the situation. The planet of pigment was suspended from a huge iron girder, and was so gargantuan that a paint roller affixed to a long stick was required to reach its poles. A mirror had been placed on the ground below it to enable proper viewing while painting the nether regions.

Mike Carmichael, the man behind this record-breaking under-taking, shook our hands and enthusiastically answered our barrage of questions. The obvious came first.

"How many?" 21,822 coats.

"How much?" Over three thousand pounds.

"Why?" It just sort of happened.

Turns out there was never any grand plan to create this colossus; it started with a happy mishap back in 1964. Mike and a high school buddy were tossing around a baseball when an errant throw landed in a can of paint. This got Mike to wondering, *What would it look like if I added a bunch of coats to the baseball, then cut the whole thing in half?* He just wanted to see the rings, like on a tree.

Neighbors and kinfolk encouraged him to add more and more lay-ers, but as the paint ball grew, they began to lobby against splitting the paint-clad sphere. Years passed and Mr. Carmichael found himself with a massive orb hanging from a chain in a spare bedroom.

"Did your wife mind?" I asked, looking out the window at Mrs. Carmichael celebrating Mother's Day surrounded by her grand-children.

"Not a bit." Mike smiled. "Glenda has added over eight thousand layers herself."

After years of keeping his masterwork strictly among family and friends, Mike felt the need to reveal it to the world. A pavilion, sponsored by Sherwin-Williams, was built to showcase the ever-growing globe, and the accolades soon followed.

Relocating the seven-foot sphere meant knocking out a wall of the Carmichael home and utilizing a forklift for the jaunt to the more fitting domicile. In doing so Mike proved the theory, "if you build it, they will come."

By no means are visitors to Mike's masterpiece a rarity. Thousands of people, from at least twenty-five countries, have made the pilgrimage to add their coats of paint and receive a certificate commemorating the event. One layer even included a marriage proposal (she said yes!).

The ball has been featured in *The Guinness Book of World Records*, on *Ripley's Believe It or Not*, and on several television networks. The walls of the pavilion are papered with photos of dozens of celebrities who have stopped by to pay homage and add a coat. *The David Letterman Show* made arrangements for Mike to bring the ball to their studios, but Mike declined, feeling that the behemoth must be seen in its proper home. Besides, you never know what might happen if a ton and a half of dried paint was turned loose in the Big Apple.

After we had viewed every angle and discussed every aspect, Mike finally uttered the words that David and I were dying to hear.

"What color do you want to use?"

With a quick scan of the dozen or so vats of paint, we grabbed our rollers and lovingly added layer number 21,823, in red. Once our coat was completed, I hand-painted a lovely Mother's Day stick figure tribute to our children, right on the globe's equator. I believe even Mike, who had seen most everything paint related in his time as curator, may have been tearing up.

Feeling the pride of being new world record holders, we contently walked away with our souvenir paint chip, the official Certificate of

Coat #21823, and a commemorative T-shirt. As we made our way back to BAMF, I turned around and shouted to Mike one last question.

"What's your regular job?"

"I'm a painter."

Perfect.

14
We're Too Old for This Crap

I might superglue myself to an overhead light fixture now and then, but I'm not stupid, and I'm not deaf, or blind . . . yet.

I could see that Veronica was obviously having issues transitioning into our new lifestyle. The Ball of Paint certainly helped distract her, but that was more than likely a temporary reprieve. She has always had a house, a sanctuary where, even if I was out on the road, she had the kids, a family, and that made it her home. Now she was going to have to come to terms with cutting those ties.

I must admit, I certainly found comfort in having a hearth and home myself, but the adjustment would be much less difficult for me, since I had traveled relentlessly most all of my adult life. I spent the better part of our last ten years in Nashville trying to find ways to reduce my touring commitments and spend more time at home. There were all sorts of good reasons for this, most pertaining to being a better husband and father, but there was also the reality that I felt like I was getting too old for the grind. That was a lot of the reason we ended up in St. Croix. It was somewhere I could stay put for a while.

So how was I suddenly not too old to embark on a sort of open-ended road trip? Hadn't I spent enough time in large tin cans rolling down the highway to last a lifetime?

Maybe not. With the kids grown and after a bit of a break, I felt like I was ready to do a little wandering again. My thinking was that if Veronica could come along, we could enjoy all of the good parts of life on the road and eliminate most of the bad. How great would it be to see new places together and endlessly explore just-over-the-horizon without soundchecks, setting up and tearing down the stage, or eating greasy truck stop cheeseburgers at three in the morning?

Pretty great, I'd say, and I was pretty sure Veronica would end up loving it.

Even though I was fully confident that we would wind up happily bouncing down the highway, there was a tiny voice asking questions in the back of my mind.

What about both of you living together 24-7 in a space roughly the size of a walk-in closet? Can you really spend all of your time with each other? Generally I would just tell the voice to shut up, but the fact was I didn't have the answers to those inquiries. Forging ahead was the only way to find them.

* * * * *

The maiden voyage of our new rolling home had BAMF setting a course south from the great Midwest toward Nashville, Tennessee. Music City, USA, was still home to many of our oldest and dearest friends, and two of my brothers. Several folks had even been kind enough to offer their driveways for us to "camp" in.

Veronica and I had quite a few people on our must-see list for our time in Tennessee, but a couple of guys, William and Steve, would not be on our itinerary.

We had been very close, working together in a band for many years, spending every waking moment with each other when we were on the road. I even roomed with William while we slogged through tours so grueling he sardonically dubbed them *The Death March to Bataan* and *The Bring Your Helmet Tour*, perhaps with a nod to his days in Vietnam. In the throes of these arduous excursions, William was the one who kept us laughing. The original Rockin' Hill–William.

But my last encounter with him was under less than stellar circumstances. The same with Steve. Business differences and personal problems pretty much destroyed the group, and our affinity. I wasn't planning on letting them know that we'd be in town.

But fate had a different plan. While BAMFing our way through the Hoosier state, I got a phone call. Steve had died. Wow. This guy had been a huge part of my life, but he was the kind of guy who could find the party people in a Tibetan monastery, then proceed to push the festivities to the brink of disaster. The edge was never more than a whisker away. He was also a major factor in the trials and tribulations of my relationship with William. We had been, after all, a band.

As I drove silently, my mind was jumbling crazy mixed emotions revolving around the way I left the situation with Steve and the sense of finality about it. Could things have been different? I'll never know.

After some quiet reflection and internal debate, I decided that I should, no, I *needed* to go to the service. No doubt William would be there too.

Veronica had her own issues with Steve. He had an ongoing difficulty with substance abuse and, as is often the case with addicts, the truth. That caused several conflicts between them. I did my best to overlook his shortcomings, because he was a really good drummer and business is business, but in the end, Veronica was right. Steve's destructive chaos broke up the band, ended our friendship, and finally took his life. She didn't want to go to the memorial, but relented, as a favor to me.

When we walked into the service, I saw William for the first time in over ten years. I was more than a little nervous, but my fear melted away as soon as he reached out to greet me.

"Hey man, good to see you. How's it going? Don't give me that handshake crap, c'mere."

Hugs were required with William. He was the same old character. If he felt any tension, he sure didn't let it show. Within a few minutes we were right back to our old selves. It turned out neither of us harbored any hard feelings.

Once we'd caught up, exchanged pictures of the kids, and reminisced about Steve, I mentioned that I had been a little anxious about seeing him. William shot that right down.

"David, when we get to our age, it's just not worth worrying about crap like that anymore."

Truer words could not be spoken. We have years of friendship and good times to look back on. Why dwell on the rough patches?

I think the ability to overlook differences is an invaluable part of getting a little older. After putting a few decades behind us, hopefully we've learned to let bygones be bygones, and not manufacture troubles. We can look for reasons to be petty, get all "Why haven't you kept in touch more?" or "I'll never forgive you for . . ." or we can be thrilled to see an old buddy and overlook the conflicts. Fortunately, William and I chose the latter.

We fell right back in with all of our truly dear friends in Nashville because all of our shared experiences, good and bad, have formed lasting relationships. From those mutual histories, we recall and retell events, and even embellish them into tall tales. That way, "Remember that time we . . .?" invariably ends up in guffaws of crazy laughter.

My old comrades-in-arms and I tend to gravitate to war stories from the road. For Veronica and her compadres, the conversations usually wind up recollecting zany antics involving kids and the times they scared the bejesus out of their parents.

Sure, *now* it's okay to laugh about the crazy night when Decibel destroyed her tibia falling from a playhouse, since she is perfectly ambulatory twenty years later. But at the time, our friend Anna, who was babysitting and had no way to contact us because we were attending a pre–cell-phone-era wedding, didn't find the situation terribly amusing. The kind of fear she felt when dealing with a crisis like that, and the relief we all felt once it was over, really cemented our friendship.

And we managed to find a comical upside. We got to watch a four-year-old crab-scoot around on her butt in a radiation-green, hip-to-toe cast for several weeks. Now *that's* entertainment.

15
The Plan Is No Plans

From Nashville, the next stop on our long-overdue-for-a-visit list would be Veronica's dad and his wife. I never really knew what to call my father-in-law until we had kids of our own. The problem was solved by The Piglet dubbing him G-pa Larry. Back when we still lived in good ole Music City, G-pa and his lovely bride, Kathleen, became Veronica's nearest kinfolk when they pulled a reverse *Beverly Hillbillies* move from Los Angeles to the hills of Arkansas. One too many relentless rush hours led them to choose a new life raising horses on a tranquil patch of land tucked away in the serenity of the Ozark Mountains.

In keeping with our secondary directive of finding diversions along our way, we were happy to note that our route would take us right through Memphis, home of the King.

Veronica and I were married on Elvis's birthday. We're not freaks—it was a coincidence. I didn't even realize what we'd done until I woke up in a champagne haze on our wedding night with the TV still blaring, half-opened an eye, and saw thousands of fans worshiping outside the gates at the temple of Elvis, Graceland. With a coincidence like that, it seems like we should have made our own pilgrimage to the rock 'n' roll mecca at some point, maybe for an anniversary or something, but we never did. That was about to change.

The tacky opulence was overwhelming the moment we walked through Graceland's front door.

"This is fantastic," I whispered to Veronica, trying to stay beyond the earshot of the King's Loyal Subjects. "It looks like Liberace decorated the inside of *I Dream of Jeannie*'s bottle."

Veronica dubbed the living room pure *Gone with the Wind*, and I reckoned that E would have liked that description. But as we moved down the hall, into the heart of the King's lair, the feel of the house shifted from syrupy Southern comfort to sixties Hillbilly Cat. Bright colors, stripes, polka dots, and checkers. This was groovy, baby.

In the mod-styled TV room, done up in stark yellow and black with mirrored ceilings, all I could think was *shooting gallery*. The recorded tour guide in our headphones didn't mention it, but it's not a very well-kept secret that whenever something displeasing came on one of the three televisions, Elvis would fire off a few rounds into the offending tube. Rumor has it that Robert Goulet's face took quite a few slugs.

"Why would they cover up the stray bullet holes? That's what I was looking forward to seeing the most."

Did I say that out loud?

We were starting to get glares from the Loyal Subjects. That wasn't likely to get any better, since Veronica was about to go completely over the edge. Tears were trickling down her face from trying to keep her laughter at bay. She has an affinity for tacky, and Graceland was her mother lode.

"Good God! Look at the ceiling!" We had entered the Jungle Room.

The King had gone completely green-shag-carpet native from top to bottom in this tropical abomination. We were speechless at first, but then the proper description came to me.

"Tiki Tacky." Which came out funny to us, but by this time everything struck us as hilarious. I had to repeat it, several times.

A few of the slightly-less-Loyal Subjects had started staying pretty close to us, and even laughing along, so I started singing "Rock-a-Hula Baby" as we walked outside. They seemed to like it, even tried to sing along, but it threw the True Loyal Subjects off a bit. I could see them wondering, *How could a blasphemer like him know the words?*

It could have turned ugly—torches and pitchforks ugly—so before the True Loyal Subjects formed an angry mob, we slipped away from the crowd and moseyed across the street to where the King's transportation was on display. The "Flying Graceland" that Elvis named *Lisa Marie,* after his daughter, was a state-of-the-art long-range jumbo jet in its day. Just a few minor modifications, like gold-plated sinks, fixtures, and seat belts, plus a conference room and a giant bedroom suite made the plane fit for a . . .

"Hey honey, know what size that bed is? King-sized." No doubt I was the first clown to come up with that gem.

"Look David, it's Little Elvis." Veronica nudged me in the ribs as we walked down the steps from the plane.

A little guy about five years old, decked out in full Elvis-in-Vegas rhinestone-studded-jumpsuit regalia and carrying a little purple suitcase, was headed up the ramp for a trip on the *Lisa Marie*.

Somewhere in the deep, dark recesses of my brain I heard him say, "Thank you, thank you very much."

* * * * *

Crossing the Mississippi River into Arkansas, Veronica blurted out, "Humpback all your whales and win a free trip to Arkansas!"

She couldn't help it. Nearly two decades ago, on this very spot, an eight-year-old Decibel proudly proclaimed that nugget of indescribable wisdom from the backseat of The Whore of Babylon. At full volume. This sort of incomprehensible declaration was commonplace for Decibel. Trips were loud and weird like that with our brood.

Veronica was buried deep in a map. "Hey, we're pretty close to Hot Springs. Maybe we should stop."

"Hot Springs is no big deal; I played there a few times." I actually didn't dislike Hot Springs per se, but I was trying to keep us on course. "What do you want to go there for?"

"To take in the healing waters."

"*Take in healing waters?*" Was she serious? "But your dad's expecting us. It's out of our way."

"Wait, *really*? Out of our way? We don't have a way these days, do we? What about the-plan-is-no-plans and all that jazz?"

Right then I realized that the idea of having a way or a plan had not left my cranium completely. Hot Springs seemed to be highlighting a fundamental difference in our styles of travel. I wanted to move forward, see things, and move on to the next place. Get where we were going. Veronica wanted to take everything in, explore, and even stay a while if something struck her fancy.

I think my method stems from years of having a set itinerary on tour. Ride the bus, eat, set up, eat, clean up, play the show, tear down, pack up, eat, ride the bus. Next day, same thing, like the movie *Groundhog Day*. Spur-of-the-moment changes or hanging out an extra day somewhere were not options. There was always another show to get to or a mad dash to Nashville to spend a few blissful days at home.

This was not the first time that these differences had caused some friction. Our conflicting styles had run up against each other in Europe too, and this time wouldn't be the last. It wasn't the end of the world or anything, but we both needed to give a little. I figured I should be a little more willing to move toward her position, because of the fact that we didn't have to be anywhere at any given time. It made sense for me to cool my jets a good bit. That, and I'm such a swell guy.

"I guess we could check it out," I offered. "Maybe it's better than I remember."

In reality, all I really remembered was the inside of a tour bus and a stage in some theater, or horse track, or something. Surely Hot Springs had more to offer than that.

"It's not like we have to get the kids back for school. Why don't you call your dad and tell him we're going to be a day or two later?"

Veronica's dad is one of the most laid-back people I know, and was one of the few family members actively encouraging our new lifestyle, so I knew that wouldn't be a problem.

Guiding BAMF through bumper-to-bumper traffic, we inched our way onto Hot Springs' famed Bathhouse Row. These grand old spas were built over the thermal springs back in the 1800s, and folks from far

Our Family Album

The Valley Girl

The Beanpole

The Wedding

The Sharkmobile

Photo credit: Indy Stewart

Rockin' the denim tuxedo

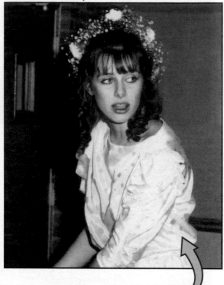

Not every gal can pull off braces on her wedding day!

David's mom

David's dad

The Piglet arrives on the scene and the Earth Mother is born

Veronica's parents——more Sonny and Cher than Ozzie and Harriet

A rare quiet moment with Decibel

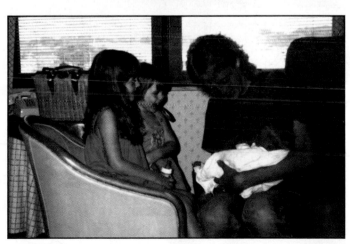

Enter The Boy

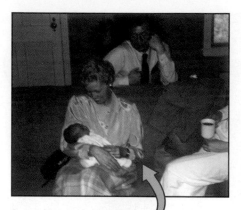

David's mom finally gets her first grandchild

Veronica's great-grandmother, of "pillowcase full of bricks" fame

Photo credit: Rowland Rushton

The best (worst?) family portrait ever!

Never a dull moment—
The Piglet, Decibel, and The Boy prepare for one of many fantastic productions

Santa Claus signs Decibel's radiation-green, hip-to-toe cast

Aviation is in The Boy's blood. He built his own flying machine at age ten.

The air up there

School student flies solo at 16

BILL KOSSLER

Photo credit: Kristin Duncan, *St. Croix Avis*

Our First Empty Nest Adventure—Italy!

Nothing like a nice piece of ass

Veronica's nemesis

David's payback,
220 volts of hair-raising fun!

Neptune's Grotto, Sardinia

Moleto, near Casale Monferrato, Italy

Press for one of the shows.
"A Disc with David James:
New project for Bonfanti"
(Il Monferrato)

Castello Dragone,
near Genoa, Italy

The Italian Riviera

The banking district in Genoa

See the USA in Your Chevrolet

You wanted to see winter

Mike Carmichael and his World's Largest Ball of Paint

The Replacement Boy made of snow, outside the dreaded orange monster

BAMF, in all his glory

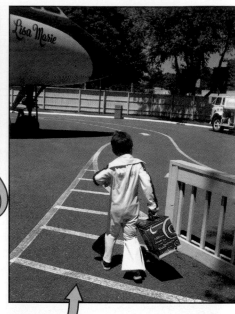

Our record-setting contribution to the ball of paint

Li'l Elvis . . . leaving the building

Women's Hydrotherapy Room, Fordyce Bathhouse, Hot Springs, Arkansas

The Quapaw Baths in Hot Springs, Arkansas

Show Me a Sign

Your ransom has been paid, ribs cost extra

Saw this and had to stop

Good thing they were "otherwise open when home"

Airing of grievances . . .

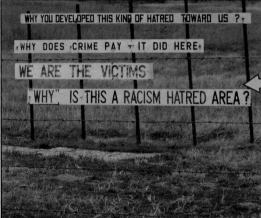

. . . Oklahoma style

Some mixed messages

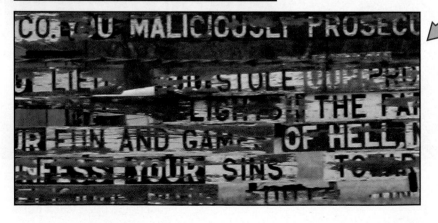

Meanwhile, in Kansas . . .

. . . Mr. Pollard has given us a lot to think about

David's Affinity for Roadside Weirdness

145-foot-long muskellunge. Those are people standing in the mouth.

World's Largest Hand-Tuned Wind Chimes

Ho ho ho. Note jolly, flesh-colored, normal-sized David below

Herding pigs at the Spam Museum

World's Largest Rocking Chair, and that's the truth

Stone sphere, for some reason said to have "a minimum value of $1,000"

Frog-shaped rock, no word on its minimum value

Yellowstone, What a Gas Hole

The Grand Canyon of the Yellowstone

WARNING

MANY VISITORS HAVE BEEN GORED BY BUFFALO

These animals may appear tame but are wild, unpredictable, and dangerous

Mind the bison!

Oh, give me
a home . . .

. . . where the
buffalo roam . . .

. . . in the middle
of the road

"Look, Mom, I'm standing on a vent that opens to the fiery bowels of the planet."

Boiling pools and geysers

Earth blowing off some steam

The Emerald Pool

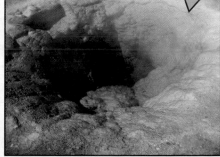

The Sapphire Pool

Fear Conquering

Veronica dressed for success

White-water rafting in Montana

I Dare Ya to Eat This!

No way were we driving past this!

Rocky Mountain Oysters after . . .

. . . and before, at which point David wished we had driven past

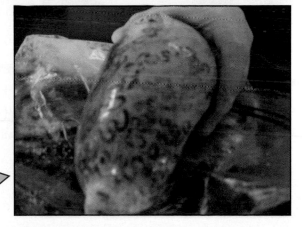

They're both "Olde World" and "Deli"

Fatball in its natural habitat, among the tulips

Fiery hot quahog

Triple D cheese-burger, deep-fried, bun and all

Poutine: cheese curds, french fries, gravy—what's not to like?

Silk worms, the worst thing we have ever put in our mouths

Cuy, guinea pig, a common dish in the Andes

Served teeth and all

The West Coast

Sporting crab headgear
at the Crab Festival

Veronica caught
this guy wild,
right out
of the tank

Served as fresh
as it gets

"Entering Oregon,"
David's
fiftieth state

The redwood forest
home of the Ewoks,
where Star Wars
was filmed

David, inspecting a redwood:
all clear,
no elves in this one

Yosemite from the tunnel entrance on State Route 41

Yosemite Falls

Full moon rising over Half Dome

Warning: Black Bears

If you encounter a black bear, do not approach it but aggressively try to scare the bear away immediately. Follow these instructions.

Yell, clap hands, bang pots, throw sticks or small rocks toward bear

Stand together to present a more intimidating mass

Do not surround the bear

Do not try to retrieve objects

Be cautious if you see cubs; their mother may aggressively defend them

Report all sightings to a ranger

Warnings about bears . . .

WARNING
This could happen to
your vehicle!

*. . . come in
all forms . . .*

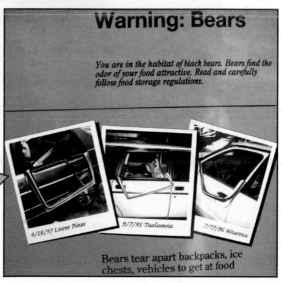

Warning: Bears

You are in the habitat of black bears. Bears find the odor of your food attractive. Read and carefully follow food storage regulations.

4/28/97 Lower Pines

9/7/95 Tuolumne

7/17/96 Wawona

Bears tear apart backpacks, ice chests, vehicles to get at food

*. . . throughout the park,
and turned out
to be necessary*

Rocks at Big Sur

Keep your eyes
on the road or . . .

McWay Falls,
Big Sur, California

Where Do We Go Now?

The cliff dwellings
of Montezuma's Castle
in Arizona

The Petrified Forest

Standin' on the Corner
in Winslow, Arizona

Organ Pipe Cactus National Monument

Sundown in the Sonoran Desert

Mexican Therapy

The tiny border crossing of Gringo Pass

The journey lived up to this promise

Parked BAMF right on the beach

One of many waterfront establishments in Puerto Peñasco

The beach where we made up our minds to Go Gypsy once and for all

and wide came to partake in the perceived therapeutic properties of the 140-plus-degree healing waters. They still do.

The Fordyce Bathhouse lodges the headquarters of Hot Springs National Park and a museum that captures the grandeur of a by-gone era. With a handy map from the front desk, we followed the self-guided tour. The first floor featured locker rooms, bathtubs, and showers, and ended up in a giant public bath complete with cheesy, Greek god–style statues and a stained glass ceiling. It was all very Victorian.

But upstairs, things took a turn for the macabre. Back in the day, some "doctor" decided that healing water alone just wasn't good enough. Nope, tools—scary tools—were invented to supplement the therapeutic powers of the springs. We had entered what looked like a Frankenstein movie torture chamber. Though we were mortified by the collection, we just had to look.

"Good God, that one has an electric plug!" came flying out of my mouth.

Our fellow tourists looked over, unsure if they really wanted to witness the quasi-medical monstrosity I had spotted. There was a smattering of nervous laughter as their eyes found the offending instrument, but real horror was the overriding emotion of the moment.

I didn't even want to think about what a foot-long glass tube with a 120-volt cord sticking out the back would be used for, especially in such close proximity to so much water.

I felt myself moving away, a strictly reflexive action. My body's neuromuscular systems were instinctively reacting to prevent any un-wanted insertions, but Veronica stood frozen by fear, curiosity, or maybe astonishment.

She had to be a little scared; we all were. But what I found waiting for us next, in the Women's Hydrotherapy Room, was really going to strike some terror into her. The contraption confronting me looked like it should be on top of a fire engine.

"Oh honey, come over and see this thing," I called out in my most amicable, singsong tone.

Wow, I'm mean.

She rounded the corner and let out a panicky little squeak when she came face-to-face with a Volkswagen Beetle–sized box containing several firehose-like nozzles protruding from one side, and a bevy of levers, knobs, pedals, valves, gauges, and dials on the other.

The whole room was tiled and waterproofed, so obviously the idea was to soak down the patient until whatever was afflicting her drowned or begged for mercy. Hey, I'd have been begging as soon as the good doctor touched that first knob.

If this was the stuff they showed to the public, I could scarcely imagine what was behind some of those locked doors. I wasn't about to stick around to find out.

"Oh gee, look at the time, we ought to get going," I muttered anxiously.

Veronica didn't take much convincing. She beat me to the door.

* * * * *

With our mineral bath detour out of the way, we proceeded up into the hill country of the Ozarks. G-pa Larry bought the farm—no, not like that—when he moved to the outskirts of Mountain View, Arkansas, about twenty years ago to set up shop as a gentleman rancher. At the time, I gave the city slicker about six months before he and Kathleen were back in Southern California. I just couldn't see how they would replace season tickets to the Dodgers and Lakers with Little League and high school hoops, or a night at the opera with bluegrass on the town square. Obviously I was way off.

As they settled in, Kathleen worked to establish the first local Girl Scout troop, animal shelter, and 4-H chapter, while G-pa became a fixture at sporting events, concerts, and community causes. They assimilated into the rural environment, even if they didn't exactly fit the mold of your typical hillbillies. They're more like old hillhippies, of which there are also quite a few scattered around the hills and hollows (that's pronounced hollers 'round here, mind you).

We used to come up from Nashville every year, but because of our island relocation, we hadn't been in this neck of the woods for quite a spell. We love it because this is one of those unique places in America that has fought to preserve its character in the face of the fast-food and Walmart invasion. While those do exist, they have not managed to vanquish the ma-and-pa cafés, craft shops, and antique stores.

In the Ozarks, antiques are interesting phenomena, a spectacular example of how one man's trash is another man's treasure. As a wise old G-pa once said, the redistribution of junk has become an integral cog in the mountain economy.

We weren't in the market for any antiquities, trash, treasure, or otherwise, but we were happy to have a bit of time to stay in one place for a few days and reconnect with family. Veronica was experiencing complete comfort with being an adult kid visiting a parent's home, or at least parked out by the barn, when a heapin' helping of helicopter mom withdrawals hit her head-on.

16
Helicopter Mom, You Are Grounded

"A mother is only as happy as her saddest child." A close friend's grandmother used to say that. When I first heard it, all three of my children were young and safely in the nest, so I could totally relate.

It wasn't until my first baby uttered her first cry that I fully understood what a heartstring was. Before that day in the hospital, the moment I first heard her tiny little voice wailing at the indignity of being taken from my womb, I was under the misguided illusion that somehow heartstrings were connected to joy and contentment. During my pregnancy I assumed that the first time I would feel their tug would be when my baby smiled at me.

That's not the way mommies are wired. If they were, it could be months before the string that binds mother and child was connected heart to heart. Unless one of those funny little infant gassy smiles did the trick.

No, the heartstring is woven instantly, left intact even as the umbilical cord is cut and, though invisible, is formed from a substance stronger than mankind will ever conceive on its own. Even though this tie is born of emotional pain, the pain of separation, what is fashioned out of a first cry cannot be broken by any force, natural or supernatural.

That attachment allowed me to instantly forget the pain of childbirth. I wanted to snatch my crying child from the doctor's hands because in that instant I knew, without a doubt, what my child needed. I alone held the secrets to my child's safety and happiness.

Our generation raised children in a different manner than our predecessors. We tended to hover over our children. We had heard too many stories of molesters among us, poison in Halloween candy, and strangers waiting to coax our babies into their cars. Gone were the days of roving packs of neighborhood kids playing outside until the streetlights came on. No longer were mothers heard shouting from front porches to call their children in for dinner.

I don't believe that dangers to children are a new phenomenon. They just became more exposed, out in the open—and we talked about them amongst ourselves and with our children. We chose not to sweep things under the rug as was done in my mother's day.

My mother and her friends would often stop off at a local appliance store on their way home from school. The proprietor allowed them to watch television as a treat, since most families didn't have sets of their own. He was a well-respected and established businessman in the neighborhood, and parents had no reservations about allowing their kids to have a little TV time after school.

When my mother came home one day and broke down, telling her grandmother that this man was touching the girls in ways she didn't understand, she was told it was a very bad thing, was forbidden to visit the store, and was never to speak of it again. Mom was spared the shame of what would likely have been a horrific public humiliation in her day, but lived her entire life under a cloud of guilt. She never fully comprehended that she shared no responsibility for the incident and was right to speak up. No one explained that her actions may have saved a large number of girls the pain of what she went through. I was in my thirties before she felt safe enough to tell me the story. In my eyes, she was a hero; yet in her own eyes, she was still some sort of fallen woman.

Her grandmother, my great-grandmother, against the societal conventions of the time, didn't exactly sweep everything under the rug, though. Tough-as-nails, she had emigrated from Bohemia alone at nineteen and, by my entire family's recollection, was both a saint and the meanest woman you'd ever come up against. And you'd better not forget about the saint part or she would knock the fear of God into you. Right upside your head.

The proprietor learned the hard way that he had picked the wrong kid to mess with. A week or so after the incident, my great-grandmother invited him over for coffee, ostensibly as a thank-you for the kindness he'd extended to her granddaughter and the other neighborhood children. He was greeted at the door by a four-foot-ten sweet little old lady with a pillowcase full of bricks. She proceeded to beat the devil out of him.

* * * * *

I more peaceably dealt with the dangers my children faced by becoming a helicopter mom. Their early childhoods were spent under my careful watch. No roaming the neighborhood allowed. They had a big fenced-in yard, and friends came to our house to play. As they got older and their horizons expanded, I made sure to befriend each of their friends' parents. Soon we became a troupe of helicopter mommies and monitored our children's progress together. It seemed we all had parents or in-laws who told us we were being overprotective, but we knew we were right. Our heartstrings told us so.

I had two teens and a tween when we moved to St. Croix, and the timing was good. In Nashville, I was no longer able to keep tabs on the kids the way I used to, and wanted to. They were in three different schools and their activities had me driving for hours every afternoon.

I had the added responsibility, and honor, of taking care of my grandfather in Cleveland and trying my best to help out with my dying mother in California. There just wasn't enough of me to go around, not in the way my immediate family was used to, or as I was used to. I look back at that period of my life and shake my head. How did I do it all?

Moving to the islands was a lifesaver. The smaller school situation fit our family's needs—and allowed me to hover in the manner to which I was accustomed. We were a close-knit community at the school; we watched out for each other. The parents knew the other families' rules—and let each other know if a youngster stepped over the line. If a mother didn't find out that her kid was messing up by being told straight-out, she could always rely on gossip. Gossip was never in short supply on St. Croix.

* * * * *

I had the notion that once The Spawn were grown, my helicoptering would abruptly come to an end. It didn't.

Trouble finds a way into everyone's lives—and as much as we hate it, trouble finds our adult children. Whether it rears its ugly head in a personal relationship, at work, or at school, it was challenging for a recovering helicopter mommy like myself not to want to swoop in and fix everything. I had to learn the hard lesson that I couldn't.

My first attempt at non-hovering was a bad breakup The Piglet went through back when she was in college. Sending the firstborn out of the nest was hard enough. Keeping my nose out of her business was even harder.

The Piglet had her first real relationship while in her freshman year. It was serious enough that the boyfriend was brought home to meet the parents. When it fell apart, it fell apart bad. The Piglet was in no mood to spill her guts, and I'm pretty sure I did an adequate job of suppressing my desire to pry. I don't know the gory details to this day, but I got the feeling she was more mad than hurt.

Because I wasn't privy to the facts, as a mother, I envisioned the worst. My worries grew weightier with every scenario I conjured up. Was she crying in bed alone? Were her friends being supportive? Was she eating? Did I need to fly up there and club the boyfriend like a baby seal?

It turns out she handled it well and has learned from the experience. Her criteria for a suitable companion are more defined. She sees relationship warning lights more clearly. She grew by leaps and bounds. These are lessons she would not have learned if I had been there clubbing the seal.

Our middle child, Decibel, was a disaster with money. She couldn't save it. This was not a good combination with the feast-or-famine income of a New York City freelance artist–type. Frankly, the whole situation scared the tar out of me.

Decibel went to theater school in the city, fell in love with it, and proclaimed she would never leave. She was hit by the you're-an-adult-now freight train upon finishing school. Suddenly she was on her own monetarily, and New York City is *expensive*! Add to that a toxic job market with a tanking economy, and things were scary and bleak indeed.

Not long after her graduation, we were hit up for a loan. Decibel knew our policy. We raise you, we put you through school, and then it's time to grow up. Period. For her to ask, I knew she was swimming in dire straits. It was *so* hard to say no. It's a lot more difficult to enforce a policy than to make one. When the abstract became a reality, my mettle was seriously tested.

As she told me how lean things were, I heard myself producing gems like "get a second job" and "maybe you should move to a less expensive city," when I really wanted to say, "honey, I'll be right there and we'll work this out together," or the more dangerous, "how much do you need?"

I stayed strong; caving in was simply not an option. Decibel was devastated by conversation's end. I hung up the phone and burst into tears. I was in a funk for a good long time. Sometimes parenting really sucks.

But she did go out and get a day job she hated, and continued to freelance. Now, years later, she is well established in her field. To my knowledge, she never went flat broke again. Going hungry can be a compelling teacher.

I thought my helicoptering instincts were in check by the time The Boy left for college and we had become full-fledged empty nesters. After all, I had been parenting adults for half a decade by then; surely I had to have learned *something*.

My initial test with The Boy came during his summer session exams after his freshman year. He was working toward his commercial pilot's license, with FAA tests coming up, when he called us at G-pa's to tell us he had the flu. Not just any flu, either; he had the swine flu. My whirlybird instinct went on immediate red alert.

* * * * *

"Homebase, this is Helicopter One. Do you read me?"

"Go ahead, Helicopter One."

"I've got a situation here. College kid with swine flu, big exam coming up. I'm gonna need to go in for some serious hovering."

"Copy, Helicopter One, but let's think about this before initiating hovering maneuver . . ."

"Nothing to think about, Homebase. Sick kid, big test, I'm going in. Engaging buttinski missiles to counter possible none-of-my-business defense systems."

"Helicopter One, Helicopter One, do not engage buttinski missiles, repeat, do not engage buttinski missiles!"

"Must engage, must engage . . ."

"No, Helicopter One, pull up, pull up! Do you read me? Pull up, before it's too late!"

* * * * *

Trying to comfort a sick child from a distance is typically enough to launch the strongest of mommies into a funk, but my gloom was elation compared to how The Boy was feeling. Couple the flu with getting a poor grade on a crucial exam *because* of the flu, and he was inconsolable.

In his weakened state, he saw no light at the end of the tunnel, and nothing I said made him feel any better. As a matter of fact, I sensed that I was making things worse.

It's hard for me to connect with The Boy. His older siblings are girls, and I know how to talk girls off a ledge. Heck, I usually have them laughing at the situation by the time we're done.

Not so with The Boy. Maybe it's because he's not as emotional in the first place, but he's just not a talk-it-through kinda guy. At least not on my timetable.

Because I *am* a talk-it-through kinda gal, there was added mommy stress in this disease debacle. I felt completely unhelpful and helpless.

I tried every angle I could think of on The Boy, but all of my "this won't seem so bad in a couple of weeks" and "let's walk through the situation together" lines sounded ludicrous as soon as they spilled out of my mouth.

Then it hit me like an I-don't-need-you-Mommy ton of bricks; The Boy *wanted* to work things out on his own! My oversupportiveness was hindering his progress, and he was too nice (or too sick) to tell me to shut up and go away. Wow, no more kissing his boo-boos for me.

Hmmm . . . could this mean I was being a hovercraft just to make *myself* feel better? If it is true that a mother is only as happy as her saddest child, was I just trying to fix my own situation?

Oh my God, is this what meddling is?

Jeez. How in the fudge am I supposed to know the difference between helping and meddling?

I needed to get away from everyone, clear my head, and blow off some steam. So I hitched a ride with G-pa into town to hit a gym and think on the treadmill while he ran some errands. I had the settings cranked up to heavy sweat and was just beginning to convince myself that I wasn't a meddler.

However, as soon as I looked up, the TV broke in with one of those dreaded *News Special Report* graphics and ominous music. Never a good thing, it always makes my heart skip.

My mind raced back to the last time a special news bulletin broke in when I was working out.

* * * * *

Back in 2009, I watched from a treadmill in Generic Midwestern College Town as the news hit that an airplane had just crash-landed in the Hudson River. People were standing on the wings and boats were circling. Oh no! The Piglet and Decibel lived in New York City, and I hoped against hope that they were all right. My first thought was to go get my phone out of the locker room to check on them.

No! I scolded myself. *Of course they are okay. They weren't on the plane and there is no sane scenario that puts either of them in the middle of the Hudson River for a plane to land on top of them.*

So I stayed put, sweat some more, and watched the news. I wondered if The Piglet and Decibel knew this was happening.

I started to wonder if I should take a little break and call them, just to talk about it. They could be scared. My inner chopper pilot made a break for her battle station.

No. Helicopter One, stand down, I repeat, stand down. Absolutely no missions will be flown today.

I forced myself to finish the workout. By the time I did, I was calm and mentally relaxed. I hit the showers.

While I was getting dressed, I pulled my cell phone out from my backpack and looked down to see a text message The Piglet had sent about two hours earlier:

"Plane crashed into the Hudson. Decibel and I are fine."

After toweling the sarcasm off of my phone, I realized I am truly a dork.

* * * * *

I don't even remember what the breaking news bulletin at the gym where Dad dropped me off was about. My mind was elsewhere. Must not have been as important as my aspiring pilot with swine flu. But I do remember the lesson I learned from the landing on the Hudson. There's only so much any parent can do from a distance, and much of it can be counterproductive.

So even with a disease attacking my youngest, I needed to manage to offer encouragement, and a little bit of mommy lovin', without falling back into dorkville. That's not meddling, or chopper piloting; it's simply remaining a mother even after The Spawn have grown.

While driving back to the ranch with G-pa, my revelation continued. My dad, who in no way could have been considered a helicopter parent when I was a child, has really become a role model for me as a parent of adult kids. He only gives advice when I ask, he never butts his nose in where it doesn't belong, and, rather than pointing out my faults, he lets me know how proud he is of my accomplishments.

Admittedly, in my twenties I viewed my father's philosophy as disinterest. Now, with a little age on me, I see its brilliance. As much as he may have wanted to meddle in my life to make himself feel better, he wisely stepped back and allowed me the privacy to work things out on my own.

Over time, the gift of allowing me to grow into myself independently has only strengthened our relationship. We have grown into much more than a father and a daughter. We are friends who enjoy, cajole, needle, and respect each other. Even more, we are adult friends who love each other truly like family.

We can now advise one another and value the advice without feeling trod upon, disagree but consider the arguments without malice or fear of hurting each other's feelings, pontificate, listen, and laugh. A lot.

Come to think of it, since I became an adult, each time I see my dad, we grow a little bit closer. It's a relationship to aspire to with my newly full-grown Spawn.

I may even adopt his signature tagline, the last thing he always says to me:

"I love you, baby. Avoid evil."

17
Home, Home on the Strange

As serene as life in BAMF parked beside the barn at the Arkansas homestead was, we still had a big bunch of kinfolk to drop in on and a long stretch of highway to get to them. The time had come to resume our travels.

There was something that struck me when we got back out on the highway. Since embarking on our friends and family visitation voyage, signs had become a big part of our new life. While I navigated and David drove, the messages that whizzed by BAMF's windshield provided a constant source of information and amusement. They proved useful for knowing where we were, how far we had to go, when we might find gas or food, and what highway to take, but on the back roads of the Ozarks, the signs took on a distinctively different flair. They announced all sorts of curiosities along the way.

This one certainly caught our eye:

WELCOME
TO
TOAD SUCK
AR

Or in case we were feeling hungry or hellbound, there was:

SMOKIN' HILLBILLY
BBQ
3MI AHEAD ON LEFT

emblazoned on a sign that shared space with this message:

YOUR RANSOM

HAS BEEN PAID BY

THE LORD JESUS CHRIST

CHOOSE HIM NOW!

Up the road a piece, we passed another sign:

SNAKE WORLD

EXHIBIT

OPEN WEEKENDS

OTHERWISE

OPEN

WHEN HOME

CLOSED

WHEN GONE

Tough to argue with that logic.

And every so often we were warned:

CROOKED AND STEEP

NEXT TWO MILES

DRIVE WITH CARE

The road certainly fit the description, and BAMF was laboring up the hills, but since this was the only way out from Dad's place heading west, we forged ahead.

By the time we crossed over into Oklahoma, we thought we'd about seen it all sign-wise. Nope, we'd barely scratched the surface. We were entering a whole 'nother dimension of billboard communication, the handwritten rural rant.

About four miles outside of Perry, we came upon the Nemechek Farm. It would seem that David Nemechek has a bone to pick. For forty years, Mr. Nemechek has exercised his freedom of speech in a most unusual way, erecting dozens of huge, eye-catching, almost pop art–styled signs protesting what he sees as a racial attack against his family and livestock. He is convinced that the fine folks of Noble County are out for some "ethnical cleansing," through the "law discrimination" of his family and cattle.

David (my David, not Mr. Nemechek) was nervous. He grew up in Kansas and was well aware that if we ventured onto private property, prairie folks might shoot first and ask questions later. He was of the opinion that, from the looks of the display, there was a good chance the sign painter had at least one screw loose.

I could hardly wait to jump out and start snapping pics. But once outside of our vehicle, I immediately felt like I was being watched from the farmhouse, perhaps through the scope of a deer rifle. I gathered my guts and gained enough testicular fortitude to cross the highway and check out the peculiar display.

The fascinating declarations were positioned haphazardly in the yard, with lines and letters in bright mismatched colors reminiscent of ransom notes hastily pasted together from magazine clippings. Some of the signs painstakingly laid out the dates and identifying numbers of the bovine victims, calling the perpetrators "bastards," "evil inbred German religious terrorists," and "liars." None of them made a lick of sense to me. Perhaps not to Mr. Nemechek either, since he seemed to ask "WHY?" about a hundred times.

WHY, YOU AND COM-

MUNITY PROMOTING

YOUR NAMES AND

DIRTYING OUR NAME, WHY?

And . . .

WHY YOU DEVELOPED THIS KIND OF HATRED TOWARD US?

WHY DOES CRIME PAY—IT DID HERE

WE ARE THE VICTIMS

"WHY" IS THIS A RACISM HATRED AREA?

. . . . and on and on.

Sadly, most of these uniquely American works of art were fading away in the harsh Oklahoma sun, falling victim to the elements of the windswept prairie. We were lucky to be able to see them up close, venturing to do so despite a gnawing fear that we would be made to pay dearly for our curiosity. But perhaps their creator had lost the fire in his belly, because no one opened fire on us.

We may never know what really happened out there in Noble County, but we genuinely hope that Mr. Nemechek has gathered some solace from his signs.

* * * * *

Pushing on across the Kansas border, we were hoping that the strange might get dialed back a couple of notches. But no, this was, after all, the Land of Oz.

Sticking to the back roads took us through the booming metropolis of Mulvane, a sleepy little burg that would be easy to drive right through without a second thought, but for a house on the edge of town.

"Look! Check that out!" David was gesturing excitedly. His voice had a nervous edge and he was pointing at a house with:

GOD IS ANGRY

and

WHO KILLED JESUS?

emblazoned across the front in giant spray-painted letters.

I started digging out the camera and announced, "I want to get some pictures."

My door was open before we even came to a stop.

* * * * *

Veronica had obviously lost her mind. She was headed right up to the ramshackle house that had been completely covered with admonitions and revelations scrawled across every available surface. The roof, fence, porch, shed, garage, and even the truck in the driveway all served as canvases for these proclamations.

I'm not sure where her sudden burst of bravery came from, because it was pretty clear to me that a person who would cover their entire house with incomprehensible end-times graffiti like:

X-END-STOP-XX EVIL SIN DRUGS / SIN-> HELL EVER FIRE

may not be the most stable dude in Mulvane, and perhaps was not safe for personal interaction. I guess the lack of gunfire at the Nemechek farm had her feeling bulletproof.

"I'm gonna stay in BAMF with the engine running and the door open. If someone comes out, run back," I cautioned her.

"Okay, I'll be really quick."

"Good idea."

Idling at the curb, I noticed someone coming out the front door. He looked disheveled, like a large gnome who had just rolled out of bed, but, even in my paranoid state, I wasn't getting a threatening vibe. Veronica hadn't seen him yet. She was still outside the dilapidated picket fence, and her vision was confined to whatever was within her camera's lens. He was headed right for her.

I was too far away to get a good feel for his mental state, and not in the mood for taking any chances, so I decided to make a move. I tried to pull up so I could nab her if need be, but the passenger door was flopping open and low-hanging limbs were scraping the roof above. Not wanting to lose a door, or the air conditioner off of the roof, I shut off BAMF and jumped out to pluck my wife out of the possible situation. Too late—the odd little oracle beat me to her.

The spray-paint prophet didn't seem agitated, though; in fact, he was smiling. He may have been unbalanced, but if so it looked to be a cheerful unbalance. I tried to slow my stride and approach in a calm, reasonable fashion. I didn't want to spook the guy. Veronica was already engaged in conversation.

"Hey, honey, this is Ronald Pollard," she said as calmly as possible, but she was visibly shaking and wide-eyed. "Mr. Pollard, this is my husband, David."

Obviously her brave photo procurement plan hadn't included contact with the inhabitant.

"Nice to meet you," I said, shaking his hand while trying to size up the situation. What I wanted to do was say to Veronica, "Way to be quick and careful, honey."

Sporting a sunny disposition, stocking cap, and a Kansas City Chiefs sweatshirt, Mr. Pollard turned out to be a gentle, friendly fellow, very different from the impression we got from the angry rants he had festooned upon his home.

I carefully inquired about his unique residence, and opened the floodgates to some serious stream of consciousness testimony. He who has ears, let him hear!

As the creator and curator of this masterpiece, he insisted we see the work in its entirety and observe every detail. So we followed him all over his property while he proudly pointed out every inch of his painted prophecies and talked, and talked, and talked.

He explained his mysterious calling and methods. For Mr. Pollard, it seemed perfectly normal that God awakened him in the middle of the night and commanded him to arise and go forth to spray messages on the side of his house. God had a lot to say.

While his choice of media might have been unorthodox, and his messages mixed, I found myself wondering about other preachers and prophets. Did Mr. Pollard's humble circumstances or lack of a wider audience make his inspiration any less authentic? I'd be inclined to think the opposite. There seemed almost no opening for ulterior motives with this guy. He certainly wasn't in it for the money or fame, so his admonitions were likely heartfelt, his proclamations pure, and his motives genuine.

When we were finally able to politely make our exit, Mr. Pollard asked if he could pray over us. Aware that it was the gracious thing to do after such a thorough tour, and always in need of any blessing we could get, we gladly accepted. So a petition was raised for our safe travels, our country's leaders ("even the wicked ones"), and anything else that came to his mind, in a mishmash of invocations and supplications that eventually managed to end with amen.

With some shared quizzical glances, Veronica and I listened, added our amens, expressed our thanks, and bid him adieu.

Turns out Ronald had given me a gift—some good thinking material for whiling away the miles behind the wheel. One man's crazy is another's reality, and we shouldn't be too quick to pick sides in that debate. Who's to say where unconventional meets unhinged? I mean, look at us, we've chosen to live in a rolling tin can. There's not much room in there to talk about other people's quirks.

18
A Little-Talked-About Sign of Aging

Being the homebody that I was, one would think that I would have been a what-the-hell-are-we-doing mess by this juncture. Not the case. I'd simply adopted BAMF as my burrowing-in, nesty place. Much to the surprise of the folks we'd been visiting, we preferred to sleep in BAMF rather than come inside a house to join the so-called real world. With a little explaining, "all of our stuff is there," "it's our own bed," "it really is comfortable," and the like, everyone understood. Until Kansas.

David's parents, traditional and Midwestern, would have none of those shenanigans. I was to pack up my things and get myself inside like a proper lady. Once I was settled in, cocktails would be served in the living room. I've always had the sneaking suspicion that my in-laws think of me as a bit of a heathen, so I suppose my new affinity for sleeping in a gypsy wagon simply sealed the deal.

Actually, I'm being a little unfair. My mother-in-law had gone to the trouble of having the maid fix up the guest room for us, so it really would have been rude not to take her up on it.

The differences between the way David and I were raised are astounding. I'm the oldest of two, he's the next to youngest of five. This meant our parents were from two different generations; mine were more Sonny and Cher than Ozzie and Harriet. I'm pretty sure his childhood was in black-and-white, and had a catchy theme song.

His parents have been married for almost sixty years; I'd have to add all of my parents' various unions together to come close to that figure. David's mother was the traditional stay-at-home mom; mine went to work and college after the first divorce. She was very much the product of her times, a Southern California divorcée.

I had by no means grown up poor. But there is a distinct economic difference between Southern California living and smack-dab in the middle of America living. I grew up in an outrageously overpriced three bedroom house; David lived in a gigantic six-bedroom, two-story home. I had ideal weather and the Pacific Ocean; he had a nanny and a summer home in the Colorado Rockies. You get more bang for your buck in the heartland.

The funny thing is, I had no idea how David had grown up until well after we were married. The first time I saw the ol' homestead in Kansas was almost a year after our wedding, when David's parents threw a party for us. Entering Wichita, I laughed and said to David, "It looks like *Leave It to Beaver*."

I was not impressed—actually repressed would have been a better description. I felt like I had just entered a world that was thirty years behind the times.

My jaw dropped when we entered his old neighborhood. Their house was huge! Wait. What?

How could the guy who owned nothing but a couple of guitars and the old Sharkmobile in which we had driven to Nashville have grown up in this house? Maybe he had told me stories and I didn't put two and two together, but there were absolutely no overt signs in his demeanor that led me to believe that he came from *this*.

David has always said that the best thing his father did for him was to insist that he make it in the world on his own. His parents' philosophy became ours. When you turn eighteen, you are an adult. If you chose to go to college, we will help you with tuition. If not, get a job and grow up.

Almost thirty years later, I found myself sitting in my mother-in-law's now scaled-down domicile, but one that was still complete with her signature all-white living room, sipping drinks.

It's been a wild ride for David's mother and me. She's known me since I was barely an adult. I can't begin to imagine what she thought of me when we first met. I was eighteen and hadn't bathed or slept after twenty-four hours of deadheading it from California to their summer home in Colorado on my way to shack up with her musician son in Nashville. Knowing me, I was probably wearing a long flowing skirt and flowers in my greasy hair. Yet, despite what had to be obvious reservations, she was more than gracious.

I was welcomed into their eclectic little ranch house, a launching point from which their children spent summers hiking, camping, and enjoying a respite from the heat of Kansas. The closest town was about eight miles away and had a population of about five hundred hippie types—including a commune. I found the place fascinating; a place to kick off your shoes and run free.

Things were different in Wichita. While the amazing graciousness remained, it was a world of customs I didn't understand, roles I wasn't used to playing, and expectations I, frankly, didn't feel the need to meet. This led to quite a bit of head-butting between my mother-in-law and me.

Sitting across from her in her beautifully decorated living room three decades later, I found myself impressed at how far we'd come. I'd learned to feel comfortable eating snacks over a white carpet, and she'd learned not to flinch when I wiped my cocktail-sauced face on her lace throw pillows.

The next morning, I woke up in a nonmotorized bedroom for the first time in over a month. It took me a few disconcerting moments to figure out where I was, and a few more beats to pick out a mental path across the dark, shades-drawn room to the bathroom. Nature was groggily calling.

Opening the bathroom door, I was instantly blinded by the morning sun streaming through an open window. I stumbled backward. It was more than the sun that was shining; there was an additional tangible, supernatural radiance. The bathroom was actually covered floor-to-ceiling with gleaming crucifixes.

David's mother, an avid collector, and the most devout, proud Irish Catholic on the planet, had really outdone herself. This was my first visit since the in-laws sold the home that David grew up in. In the downsizing, it looked as though every crucifix—and there were many—that had adorned the walls of their sprawling, five-kid-raising previous home had been hung lovingly in this tiny bathroom of their new pared-down empty nest house.

I almost wet my jammies in the midst of all this God-glow. Luckily, I got to the toilet in time—though peeing, even in the proper receptacle, was a tad upsetting in this most holy of bathrooms. I closed my eyes for the duration.

After I finished up the task at hand, I unclenched one eye and peeked at my surroundings. It felt like hundreds of suffering Jesuses were peering down upon me. There were crosses in every style imaginable, from shiny South American pounded metal to the more traditional old rugged wooden ones. I could feel the guilt of my Catholic upbringing welling up in me. The time had come to take stock of myself.

All the crucifixes in the world couldn't prepare me for what I found when I looked the mirror. *I had an eyebrow on my eyelid!* And it was a honker. Browbeating me, as it were.

Let me clarify a bit. My newest brow tress was situated on the lid that covers my eye when I blink. This position gave the little devil the demonic advantage of not being visible when I had looked in the mirror with my eyelids open. I was blind, but now I saw. The perfect union of sleepiness and guiding light had allowed me to witness what must have been obvious to the rest of the world for Lord knows how long.

Here's the thing: my best features come from my Romanian roots. I've always enjoyed having dark hair and blue eyes. I am psyched that my "gray" hair is silver—some people pay big bucks for that. Dracula was Romanian, and by most accounts was a particularly handsome man-thing.

That being said, we Romanians are a very hairy people. Not only did my beloved Grandpa have follicles growing out of his ears, but in his later years his lobes looked like small woodland creatures. My stunningly gorgeous mother had quite the collection of creams, bleaches, waxes, and other tortuous means of ripping hair out of unwanted locations. Luckily, I have a dash of the less hirsute Western European DNA in the mix, so I don't look like Cousin Itt. Yet.

Armed and ever aware of my Romanian hairy heritage, I remain on steadfast lookout for the inevitable mustache, the gratuitous nose whisker, or the stray fur–bearing mole. I've been beating back a unibrow since puberty. I am immune to the pain of tweezers. But as the years have passed, I've been forced to employ magnifying reading glasses to keep up my persistent plucking practice. Seeing is a top priority while I keep unruly outgrowths at bay.

This particularly strong-willed stray had cleverly chosen an impossible-to-tweeze spot. This fact did not divert me from the task at hand though. The sucker had to be plucked, even if it took a miracle. I didn't think it would come to that, but at least I was in the right bathroom should the need arise.

In order to get close enough to the mirror for my assault, I donned my eyeglasses, hoisted one knee up on the vanity for hands-free support, and leaned in at a vertigo-inducing angle. I could feel the Jesuses wondering what I was up to. I silently beseeched them for a little guidance.

With one eye closed, clutching the tweezers in my right hand, I used my left forefinger to gingerly reach behind the lens of my glasses whilst trying not to leave a view-obstructing smudge. I could therefore elevate my upper lid high enough to see the offending hair. Unfortunately, this feat prevented any light from coming in from above, divine or otherwise, seriously impeding my efforts. The thought of pinching even a teeny part of my eyelid with the tweezers during the yanking procedure promptly precipitated my aborting the mission. The danger of foul verbal discharges was just too great. If I cussed in this bathroom, I was likely to be smote.

Three more eye-wateringly unsuccessful attempts and I had resigned myself to the fact that the obstinate sucker was never coming out. I was destined to go through the rest of my life with a marmot covering my left eye. Maybe I should just treat it as a pet and name it. Problem is, the only moniker I could come up with should not be repeated in mixed company.

Especially not in front of all of these Sons of God.

Or my in-laws.

19
Help! There's No One to Eat the Leftovers

Seeing so many folks over a fairly short time had confirmed the validity of our idea to get a motor home. Visiting the people we hadn't had a chance to spend quality time with for ages, enjoying the cheesy diversions along the way, and dragging the comforts of home with us wherever we happened to be was working like a charm.

So much so that after a few nights of sleeping in my parent's house, Veronica actually said, "I'm so glad to be back on BAMF."

I must admit I was surprised by that. I half expected her to be longing for a stationary domicile after a taste of homelife.

Maybe the adaptation to living in a miniature rolling house really wasn't all that difficult. Seriously, how much space did we need? Perhaps our stint in the orange grease monster condo made the transition easier, since comparatively, BAMF was Buckingham Palace.

Still, there were adjustments. One of the most vexing was something all empty nesters face, no matter where they live—cooking for two.

Throughout our nearly three decades of marriage, I have gladly done the shopping and meal preparation, at least when I was home. I actually like it. Ever since they moved out, inevitably one of the kids will call every week to ask things like "how long do you bake a chicken?" or "what's in that stroganoff you make?" or "what was that stuff you made that one time that was so good?"

About an hour and a half, Worcestershire sauce, and spaghetti carbonara.

I like to eat, so early in life I figured out how to cook the things that I wanted to consume. A natural offshoot of cooking was shopping, so

I learned to do that too. I'm such a hunter-gatherer. With three kids, I had to be.

A trip to the grocery store used to involve multiple shopping carts and severe wallet damage. By the time the cubs were teenagers, it required a small truck and a second mortgage. They were like bears awakening from hibernation, so if they chose to come along, only perfect weather, no traffic, fast driving, and sheer luck could get half of the provisions home prior to ingestion. One red light and there would be nothing left but paper products, canned goods, and empty wrappers. Even those wouldn't have survived, except that they would only eat paper as a last resort—and I had learned to pat them down for can openers.

On one of those homeward sprints, I'm pretty sure they were trying to start a fire in the back of The Whore of Babylon. It didn't smell like any of the usual burning odors that emanated from that car on a fairly regular basis, so I knew it must have been them. Luckily I pulled into the driveway before smoke began to fill the interior. The little barbarians were behind the backseat tearing open a package of meat with their teeth.

After that, I learned to check for matches, lighters, flint, sharp sticks, charcoal, grills, grates, skewers, coat hangers, and long-handled forks, even if we were just going to the Kwik Sak for gas.

So there's been a bit of an adjustment from shopping for a pack of ravenous teenaged wolves to provisioning two middle-aged wandering gypsies. Even more so when the eating habits of said gypsies are completely different from one another.

I like meat. Almost any meat. If it squeals, moos, gobbles, baas, swims, claws, or clucks, I'm all over it. Skin it, pluck it, shell it, or scale it, and lob it on the fire. Veronica calls herself a meat avoider—not an abstainer or a vegetarian, an avoider. As near as I can tell, that translates to *let me try a bite of that pork chop, it looks way better than this salad.*

She claims that this is somehow my fault. The reason I never get a carnivorous dish to myself is because I make things look so good while I'm eating them. I can't help it; I like food.

But back to the point, it's hard to find foods sized for just one or two people. Our days of the family pack side o' beef are gone. I used to celebrate finding twenty-seven pounds of Grade A beef on sale for pennies a pound. Now I get to buy one strip steak for tonight's dinner at $27.00 a pound. What a deal!

I guess I could try breaking up the giant bargain packs and freezing the portions. But, Veronica's bites as she avoids the stuff notwithstanding, how long would it take for me to go through a side of beef all by myself? Certainly longer than it takes frozen meat to turn into that strange crystallized cardboard space-food product it becomes in the freezer. Plus, half a cow would never fit in BAMF's tiny refrigerator.

On the bright side, even though bargains were no longer a part of my shopping agenda, the final bill was certainly less of a shock. Dozens of dollars instead of hundreds, I'll take that and like it. But the transition from vats of spaghetti, cauldrons of soup, and Fred Flintstone slabs of meat to dinner-for-two was far from complete.

The old habits of institutional-style meal preparation were not going down without a fight. Months into our empty nest existence, I still found myself making enough food for a small army. Leftovers became the staple of our diet. Time after time, I dug to the back of the fridge only to find some container filled with what looked to be an award-winning science fair project.

I knew there were only two of us, and that Veronica hardly eats any of the same things I do—sneak attacks from her fork notwithstanding—but I had yet to complete the reprogramming of my cooking circuits.

I decided to address this need to reboot as a challenge. A motivation to explore new culinary creations. Cooking for the brood generally wasn't fun—there was a mundane quality to the fill-'em-up-and-send-them-on-their-way fare of our full nest days—but our new mobile empty nest had none of the limitations involved in family meal preparation. This new gypsy chef had the freedom to try ingredients and whip up dishes I never would have dreamed of plopping down in front of the kids. The seafood and produce sections of the supermarket became my playground. I found myself buying things like bok choy and tilapia.

The freedom to experiment, combine interesting flavors, and incorporate Veronica's tastes into my efforts ushered in a renewed joy of cooking. I enjoyed it again, not as a task, but as a recreation. Plus, I liked getting compliments. In fact, getting compliments to the chef from my wife became my *Top Chef*–type motivator.

20
The Blowup

The next leg of our catch-up-with-everybody road trip would involve some serious mileage. Our last group of unvisited kin was my brother's family and an extended group of beloved step-relatives in Southern California, half a continent away. The most direct route from Kansas would have been through the Desert Southwest, but it was summer and the temperature out there was hovering somewhere between pizza oven and the bowels of hell, so we figured a northern tack was in order.

There were other incentives to take our modern-day covered wagon along that route —the fantastic sights of Yellowstone, Yosemite, and the Redwoods all beckoned—and since BAMF had decided not to kick the bucket on the initial chunk of our journey, we figured we'd seriously press our luck for a few thousand more miles. Do the old *See the USA in Your Chevrolet* thing. We could also cross a big item off of David's bucket list: Oregon.

David had managed to set foot in forty-nine of our fifty states during his days as a traveling troubadour. Oregon would be the last notch on his belt. He wanted to cross off the Beaver State in the worst way.

But there was a storm a-brewin' on the horizon, and it had all the earmarks of being a whopper. Looking back, I'm pretty sure our communications skills had taken a vacation when the nest emptied. We were so hell-bent on being deliriously happy that neither of us wanted to rock the boat by bringing up any irritating little things. By the time the inevitable blowup blew up, it just about blew the lid clean off.

Anyone who has been married as long as we have can attest to the give-and-take necessary for harmonious cohabitation. And with kids involved, especially considering our very different approaches to parenting (David being the far-more-reasonable counterbalance to my hovering ways), we learned that if we were not communicating properly, things could go terribly awry.

When we embarked on our new life as empty nesters, I guess we just stupidly assumed that we were in complete agreement on everything. After all, we did come up with this harebrained scheme together. We figured we had breezed right through the initial challenges that many empty nest couples encounter. It never occurred to us that we wouldn't be on the same page when it came to how we wanted to travel.

David has what I would consider a slightly less-than-healthy affinity for weird stuff. Get us within driving distance of the World's Only, Largest, Tallest, or Deepest *anything* and you can't keep him away. Because of this obsession, I've seen the World's Largest Hand-Dug Well, the World's Largest Rocking Chair, the World's Only Corn Palace, the Only Home of Throwed Rolls, the Spam Museum, the Mustard Museum, the World's Largest Hand-Tuned Windchimes, the World's Largest Ball of Twine, a Perfectly Round Rock Worth Over $1,000, and a rock that looked kind of like a frog outside of the middle-of-nowhere Oklahoma (that one wasn't valued, but I'm guessing it wouldn't go for much on eBay). We almost died crossing a horrifying wood-planked hanging bridge to get to that stupid frog. David's idea to counteract BAMF's obvious overload on the structure's questionable weight limit? Drive fast.

Ginormous fiberglass things—oh my God—the man goes crazy for them. I've seen Abe Lincoln, the Jolly Green Giant, and a Paul Bunyan all standing over forty feet tall. I've stood inside the mouth of a 145-foot fish. That behemoth was billed as a "walk-thru fish one-half city block long, four and a half stories tall, hand-sculpted into the likeness of a leaping muskellunge." I accompanied David on his pilgrimage to Sparta, Wisconsin—the mecca for formidable fiberglass figure fanatics—to see the infamous mold field of the F.A.S.T. Corporation, which stands for Fiberglass Animals, Shapes & Trademarks, and is where many of these monstrosities were born. David bounded through the acres of giant molds like a kid needing to pee on Christmas morning.

Don't get me wrong—I'm as delighted by a weird roadside diversion as the next guy. But couple David's obsession with the fact that he will drive like a maniac to get there, see it as quickly as possible, and then move on to the next shiny object, and you have a very grumpy Veronica indeed. I call his style wham-bam-thank-you-ma'am traveling.

The man also refuses to backtrack. He won't turn around under any circumstances. I'm serious—if there was a ginormous diamond-encrusted fiberglass platypus at the bottom of the World's Deepest Hole and we inadvertently whizzed by it, that's it. We missed it. I don't get it, and it drives me nuts.

I prefer to soak a place up. I had the notion that since we didn't have set plans, we could find places we liked, sit a spell, meet people, listen to accents, chill. My belief is that a place is more than just the sum total of its attractions; it's a living, breathing work in progress. I want to feel that, be a part of it.

Our conflicted state of affairs came to a head in one of our nation's greatest treasures, Yellowstone National Park.

I was feeling grouchy on our third day at the park. Deservedly so. This sea level–raised gal had hiked the crap out of the Grand Canyon of the Yellowstone the day before—at high altitude, thank you very much. I'm worthless when oxygen deprived.

My initiation into any sort of serious elevation came when I was eighteen, on my first visit to David's parents' funky little ranch house in the majestic Sangre de Cristo Mountains of southern Colorado. The place clocks in at eighty-two hundred feet. There is literally no air.

Spending the summers of his childhood at that altitude bestowed David with the lungs of a Sasquatch, so he doesn't notice the thin air. As a teenager, he logged many an hour backpacking in the mountain wilderness. Interesting conversations crop up amongst teenaged boys when they're out in the woods for weeks at a time, commonly opening with hormone-infused gems like, "What would you do if Farrah Fawcett came down the trail right now?"

After a few days, the crack of dawn wasn't safe in their presence.

David must have kept this unfulfilled wilderness love fantasy alive over the years, because on the first evening we arrived at his folks' place, he suggested we go for a little hike. Being young and ignorant in the ways of altitude sickness, I didn't hesitate to charge the mountain. Huffing and puffing—and stubborn and competitive—I wasn't about to show weakness. On top of a stunning, sunset-lit bluff, David made his move. I turned into his embrace and promptly threw up all over his boots.

Yellowstone is not quite pukingly high, but a brisk bike ride through the geyser portion of the park on day one had me realizing that a few days at a base camp would have been a good idea before attempting to hike the canyon. But in the throes of not wanting to rock the empty nest jubilation, I stupidly kept my mouth shut and proceeded into the gorge. I had hopes of it being deep enough to afford me a few extra molecules of oxygen. If it was, the difference was not something my air-starved brain was capable of noticing.

Day three dawned early as "wham-bam-thank-you-ma'am" David was up and ready to go buffalo hunting. I dragged my sore, altitude-addled self out of BAMF's loft, determined to be a good sport. I, too, really wanted to see a buffalo. We mounted our beat-up bikes—they had been hanging for thousands of dusty miles on the back of BAMF—and headed to the area of the park we deemed most likely for a sighting. I was dying. My oxygen-deprived muscles were screaming at me to cease and desist.

After huffing and puffing for about five miles, we turned a corner and were warned by an oncoming cyclist, in a very British singsongy voice, to "Mind the bison!" She sounded exactly like Mary Poppins.

Rather than heeding these considerate words of warning, I opted to focus on the humor of the phrase itself. One look at David's shaking shoulders as he pulled ahead and I knew the cyclist's warning had tickled him just as much. I summoned my waning strength and caught up to him to go in for the kill. With my last ounce of energy I yelled in a horrific English accent:

"Mind the bison!"

That did it. We were both laughing hysterically as we came out of the curve and found ourselves nose-to-nose with an enormous buffalo. Nothing like two thousand pounds of matted, ratty fur and giant horns to put a halt to the jocularity. We slammed on the brakes and hoped against hope that he was a nice buffalo. One that didn't mind the high-pitched squeal of our beat-up bicycles stopping in the nick of time. Pushing backwards up on our tip-toes—too afraid to dismount—we eased away from our hulking new friend.

"Crap, there's millions of them," whispered David, his eyes darting around in his very still head.

Looking around, I noted two things. There were indeed quite a lot of buffalo, and in the middle of the herd there was an ambulance. The rangers ride around in ambulances? I supposed it must save time. Certainly if I survived this buffalo attack I would be in need of immediate medical attention for the heart attack I felt coming on.

The tiptoeing was working. Step by tiny step we distanced ourselves from the critters. When we had retreated enough that we no longer felt hot buffalo breath on our faces, David said, "What kind of warning was that? 'Mind the bison!' How is there anyone left alive in England?"

Normally I would have found the remark hysterical. Instead, I lost it. Poor David didn't know what hit him.

"Maybe if you weren't so hell-bent on killing me, you could watch where you were going!"

"What?" He looked genuinely confused. "Where did that come from?"

Perhaps I should have calmed down and talked to him rationally. Nah.

"All we do is race full bore at everything! I don't even have time to breathe! You have got to slow down!" I yelled at the top of my nearly collapsed lungs. "Then you have the balls to blame that nice Mary Poppins lady for almost killing us? She was just trying to help!"

David just stared at me. He had avoided a collision with a large hairy mammal, only to plow straight into a hysterical wife. I saw his confusion and could have stopped and ended the tiff right there.

But then he said, "Ohhhhhh. So this is why you've been so passive-aggressive lately."

Now *that* pissed me off. He might as well have asked me if I was PMSing. I wasn't even sure what he meant, but it couldn't have been a good thing.

I got right in his face and hissed through clinched teeth, "What?" Then let fly at full volume, "*What do you mean passive-aggressive?*" followed by a syrupy-sweet sarcastic, "How am I passive-aggressive?"

Oh.

David fired back with a list of his own pent-up grievances. "Every time we try to do something, you stall as long as possible. I work it out so we can do stuff and have enough time to see everything, and you're never ready. You act like you have no idea that we're going to be somewhere until we get there. Then it's 'just a minute' or 'I have to change' or 'I want to put on makeup' or 'I need to make a phone call,' or whatever."

Hmmm, I hadn't thought of that. Though I couldn't agree that I was being purposefully belligerent, I could see his point. But I wasn't ready to give up the arguing. So I spent a couple of days toggling between petulance, pouting, and provoking. Yeah, a bit passive-aggressive.

But the more I thought about it, the more I realized that there was nothing going on in our lives that merited getting all worked up. Certainly this wasn't worth hurting each other over.

I suppose nothing ever was. Were any of the reasons for our spats through the years really worth all the anger? I don't think so now, but that's easy to say with twenty-twenty hindsight.

No doubt we were both more volatile back in our younger days. My darling husband was a yeller, but I was a thrower. At one point I think the Dodgers were scouting me. Shoes, cups, books, or whatever I could get my hands on was gonna get airborne when I got pissed off.

Good thing David was a dodger. One time I hurled an alarm clock his way by spinning it around by its cord and launching it slingshot style. Talk about a helicopter mom.

Those outbursts aside, we tried throughout our married life to avoid losing sight of the big picture and remember why we got married in the first place. We made an effort to find time for kid-less escapes now and then, even if just for a night or two, and talked. Sounds simple, but I know a whole lot of couples who just don't talk to one another about meaningful stuff.

Then they find when the chicks have flown the nest that they don't have anything in common anymore. After spending decades of living for work and the kids, they have lost track of what attracted them to each other in the first place.

We were determined not to have that happen to us, so we revisited the system that had worked so well for us over the years. We discussed our conflicting traveling philosophies in a reasonable fashion, returning to the sanity of actually talking things out instead of shouting grievances at each other.

David was already aware of his penchant for pressing forward faster than a free-spirited gypsy-type empty nester should, and he was working on it. I had to admit that, intentionally or not, I could see how never being ready until the last second might become annoying.

I guess it wouldn't kill me to put my shoes on before we stop somewhere.

21
THE Talk

Our little refresher course in communication skills did us good. Neither one of us is a skilled mind reader, so we need a good grievance airing from time to time.

Child rearing certainly helped us learn this lesson. It's why Veronica and I are a much better couple now than twenty years ago. The only way to know what's on someone's mind is to talk to them. Ask, don't guess. Relating to our kids as they got older played a big part in our grasping this.

We always tried to treat our kids like people, individuals. They were allowed to have their own ideas and thoughts. This might be due to our boomer backlash from the *children should be seen and not heard* theory of prior generations.

For instance, my mother would bristle when we asked our kids what they wanted for dinner. I'm not talking short-order cook stuff (ask for anything on the menu and everyone gets whatever they want), just a couple of choices that we would put to a casual vote. Chicken or spaghetti, guys? Winner take all. Mom thought that was way out of line.

Back when I was a kid, we all sat down together, got what was served, and liked it. Period. We were card-carrying members of the Clean Plate Club. There were starving children in China, after all.

No doubt either one of these approaches could work, or go right off the rails, depending on the participants and how far to the extreme they took it. There has to be some flexibility; that's another of the many things we learned as we went along in parenting.

One of my first big revelations as a father came after a two-hour battle with our firstborn over a carrot. Obviously I had yet to learn to pick my battles. Just a couple of years into parenthood and I set the standard for what would forever stand as the lowest point of my fathering career.

To this day I have mixed feelings about the incident. On one hand, I still think I was right about parental authority and children trying new things, but on the other, there is no doubt that I handled things in a horribly inappropriate manner. There simply isn't any valid justification for a grown man spending the better part of two hours trying to coerce a two-year-old into eating one tiny bite of carrot. No matter how frustratingly obstinate that toddler could be.

Like any new parent I felt like a *Stranger in a Strange Land*, but failed to heed Heinlein's sage advice: "*Never attempt to teach a pig to sing; it wastes your time and it annoys the pig.*"

The Piglet was in her high chair and proudly proclaimed that she had finished her TV dinner (another low point in the parental record book) when, unfortunately for both of us, I noticed that the vile little reconstituted cubes of orange cardboard on her tray had not been touched.

"You need to eat your carrots."

"I don't like them."

"How do you know you don't like them? You've never tried one before."

"I don't like them."

"Try one before you say you don't like them."

"I don't like them."

"Don't tell me you don't like them. They could taste like ice cream for all you know—now try one." I scooped up one of the little cubes with her spoon.

"I don't like them."

"Just try one, that's all, then if you don't like it, you don't have to eat the rest." I tried to move the spoon up to her lips.

"I don't like them." She squeezed out through clinched teeth. The spoon was promptly emptied, having been transformed into a vegetable catapult.

"*How do you know . . .*" I was getting fully agitated, yelling even, "*until you try one?*"

Veronica called out from the other room, "What's going on in there?"

"I don't like them."

"Nothing, honey." No need to get the wife involved.

"I don't like them."

My brain was about to explode, so I backed it down a couple notches into silent seething mode.

This would be the first of many standoffs that I would experience with The Piglet over the subsequent sixteen years. Looking back, I think I set a bad precedent right then and there, but I wasn't about to give in. As a novice in the field of child rearing, I had no idea when to make my stand, or when to simply declare victory and surrender. I was ready to go to the mat. So was The Piglet.

I tried to regain my composure. Quietly, but really pissed, I managed, "Fine, then we'll just sit right here until you try one."

"I don't like them."

How do kids ever survive to adulthood?

This had become an epic battle of wills, and it would go on and on for an amazingly long time. Stubborn didn't even begin to describe the two combatants in this altercation. At one point Veronica looked in, shook her head, and simply walked away in disgust. I heard the bedroom door shut. After another hour or so, I sat truly in awe at the display of obstinate tenacity this toddler was putting forth. Then I snapped. I'd had it.

"Okay, that's it. You *will* eat this carrot."

"I don't like them."

I went for her spoon again, but The Piglet was not about to suffer that indignity. Before I could reload the catapult, she was free of her high chair and flying out of the room. All I saw was a diapered butt bouncing into the kitchen at top toddler speed.

I sprung into action and was right behind her, cautiously balancing a couple of carrot cubes on the spoon, skillfully leaning into the curves so that centrifugal force would keep them in place, balancing with Cirque du Soleil precision, and bellowing at the top of my lungs the entire time. But The Piglet's low center of gravity and innate lack of clumsiness gave her a distinct advantage. Not once did she bang a knee on a coffee table or slam a shoulder into a door jamb while the crazed pursuit took child, father, and vegetable through every room of the house.

Finally, Veronica's panicked pleas and my mounting bruises broke the psychotic episode. I gave up.

The Piglet won, and this did not sit well with the young daddy. There were other showdowns over the years, as there should be with any healthy, intelligent kid, and we won them, as any healthy, intelligent parents should, but I couldn't help feeling that somewhere in the furthest recesses of her mind The Piglet always knew that she had won the first round.

Years, and two more offspring, taught us to understand the difference between a toddler refusing to try something new and a teenager about to try something that could have lifelong consequences. We learned where to draw the lines so that confrontations could often be avoided completely.

Some passed-over food seemed mighty inconsequential once kids were making decisions with real weight, and we wanted them to be comfortable including us in that process. We learned to encourage our kids to voice their opinions, strove for actual discussions, tried to stay engaged in their lives, and made an effort to see things from their point of view.

There were still plenty of disagreements, especially when final rulings came down. After all, we were not running a democracy. That would have been crazy. We were outnumbered! It was more like a constitutional monarchy. One where the royals maintained ultimate power.

As time went by, the ability to have real conversations came to play a huge part in our transformation from the child-parent relationship to an adult-to-adult one. But in getting to that end, there were times when a good translator would have come in handy.

The Great Puberty Wars may have been the worst of it. It was like the terrible twos all over again. Only this time we were dealing with bigger, smarter, wilier entities. Entities that were convinced we were out to ruin their lives. No matter how many times we tried to explain that our decisions were made with their best interest at heart, it didn't seem to sink into their hard little heads.

Teenagers feel that every party is the after-party at the Academy Awards, every game is the Super Bowl, and every day is their last day on earth—so denying them anything really *is* the end of the world to them.

Basic stuff like, "No, you can't go to a party at someone's house if their parents aren't home," became the Hundred Years' War. Or at least an all-night battle.

"No, you can't use the car tonight—I need it, but I'll be glad to drop you off," somehow sounds just like, "I hate your guts and want to destroy your very soul," to the ears of an adolescent.

Child rearing is a war of attrition, and we were fairly sure that if we could just hold our ground we would emerge victorious. I held onto the hope that one day my kids would see things the way I'd heard Mark Twain had:

"When I was a boy of fourteen, my father was so ignorant I could hardly stand to have the old man around. But when I got to be twenty-one, I was astonished at how much the old man had learned in seven years."

By The Piglet's senior year of high school, peace (or at least an uneasy truce) had been restored. But there was one last parting shot left in the adolescent arsenal.

"I'm eighteen now. I can do what I want."

That dreaded time when the teens are technically adults, but still in high school. At that age when they think that being an adult means the freedom to head out and start being stupid at top speed, without any of that pesky earning a living and paying bills stuff.

The standard "Not in my house" or "As long as you live under my roof, you'll abide by my rules" replies didn't gain much traction with our young 'uns. A resolution with a little more weight behind it was required.

While driving The Piglet to school one day, as she rambled on about how we no longer had any authority over her, I got fed up. I pulled into the drop-off lane and calmly laid out to her what became known in our family as "THE Talk." No, not *that* "the talk," this one:

"Yup, you're right, you are an adult, which means we are through with our job of raising you. Anything we do from here on out is as a favor to you—out of the goodness of our hearts—because we love you. Get this straight: we don't owe you anything anymore. We don't owe you a college education. We would like to help you with one, because we want what's best for you, but we don't have to. We don't owe you a place to live. We will be glad to provide one for you temporarily, until you graduate from high school, but we don't owe it to you. Don't like our rules? Fine, leave. We can't, and won't, try to stop you. In fact, legally we can kick you out of *our* house right now, today, because—oh yeah—that's right—you're an adult. There would be no repercussions for us because we're done, we did our job."

A similar version was repeated as each offspring reached voting age. Happy birthday.

Harsh, but very effective.

The results were remarkable. Almost immediately the uppity teen attitude changed. No more yelling, just a little brooding as reality set in. Then they started actually seeing themselves as adults, not just using the word as an argument to stay out all night. The understanding that real life has real consequences began to dawn on them. A bridge had been crossed. Though not as fun, this transition was every bit as thrilling to see as a toddler's first steps.

THE Talk became less harsh with each chick readying him- or herself for flight from the nest. The younger ones had the benefit of seeing their siblings go over the bridge before them. By the time The Boy was making his transition, I barely had to mention it. He knew the drill.

However, I still felt like I had one nagging piece of unfinished business as a dad. The Piglet was visiting us on St. Croix during her senior year of college, and we had developed a tradition of stopping at the Paradise Café on the way to the airport whenever she was leaving. She loved their vegetable soup. It had tons of carrots in it, but, as The Piglet had done for years, she would leave them in the bowl. She had become a carrot detection and extraction expert.

For over two decades, no stewed, boiled, shredded, pot-pied, ranch dressing–dipped, or even baked-in-a-cake carrot made it past her lips. Her stubbornness knew no bounds. She had never consumed a carrot in any form. Ever. She could find microscopic bits of them in dishes no one ever suspected contained carrots. Many a time I looked over at her plate at the end of a meal only to see a tiny pile of tuber bits gleaned from some unknown source. It wasn't like I was trying to sneak one past her. Who knew Rice-A-Roni had carrots in it?

On our way to the pre-airport lunch, she had been begging me to change her ticket so she could stay a few more days, but I was pretty sure that it would cost too much. Over her soup she continued the pleading. The Piglet is nothing if not tenacious. Suddenly, a long dormant ember sparked in the deep recesses of my mind. The statute of limitations had not run out, as far as I was concerned.

"Let me go outside and check what it costs to change your flight." I offered (cell phones didn't work inside the four-hundred-year-old brick, hurricane-proof dungeon of a restaurant). She was so happy, smugly confident that she had charmed her old dad and was going to get her way.

Until I said, "But if I change it, you have to eat a carrot."

I didn't wait for a reply. I was out the door to let her stew on it.

She must have been doing some pretty serious stewing, because by the time I got back inside, she was nearly hysterical. A grown woman bawling and causing a huge scene in a crowded restaurant. Customers were staring, and the waitress looked at me like I had been outside killing the family cat.

Sometimes it's hard to tell with The Piglet whether she is putting me on or not, but she had worked herself into quite a state. All red-eyed and trembling with fear, real fear. Carrotphobia.

I started to feel bad, like I really had scarred her for life, but I snapped out of it. Victory was too close; this was no time to go soft. I had to buck myself up so I could go through with my diabolical plan.

"It doesn't cost that much, so if you eat a carrot, I'll go back out and change the ticket."

A tiny little "Do I have to?" came from across the table. She was actually sobbing. But I refused to allow her attempts to weasel out of the bargain weaken my resolve.

"No, you don't have to. It's your choice. Leave today, or eat a carrot and stay 'til Monday."

"Okay, here goes." But she couldn't do it. She gave the little orange bit a sniff and whimpered, "I'm concerned it might be pungent."

Seriously, that is exactly what she said.

"We'd better get going to the airport, or you're gonna miss your flight."

I started to get up from the table.

"No, no, I'll do it. Do I have to swallow it?"

"Yup, but we have to go." No cracks in my armor.

She popped the small piece into her mouth and chewed between sobs. I was watching like a hawk for any napkin spitting, but she managed to gag the morsel down.

I was actually starting to feel sorry for her, she made herself so pitiful, but then I thought back twenty years and went in for the kill.

"You didn't really have to eat it, I already changed the ticket. Oh, and by the way . . ."

I inserted a long pause for dramatic effect.

"I win."

22
Lessons Learned in a Walmart Parking Lot

While the idea behind getting BAMF was to avoid going broke on our long overdue visit excursion, camping can still be a little costly. Our rolling home can seriously suck down the fuel, and RV parks generally run anywhere from twenty to fifty bucks a night.

In order to keep those expenses down, David and I quickly discovered the beauty of dry camping, often known as boondocking, by pulling off the road to sleep without any services like water or electricity. BAMF is reasonably self-contained and can provide all the comforts of home even without a campground, at least for a few days.

The most plentiful, and easiest to find, boondocking locations are Walmart parking lots. Many of the stores are open all night, have security patrols, and actually encourage overnighters. It brings in business. But it is usually just a place to spend a night and then head on down the highway. For obvious reasons, a Walmart lot is not often considered a destination.

It's rare to be the lone boondocker in a Walmart parking lot. Usually there are quite a few fellow blacktop bivouackers, but the Supercenter in Bozeman, Montana, caught us by complete surprise. We met people from all over the world in that lot. It was a veritable RV rodeo of motor homes, campers, trailers, pop-ups, buses, and trucks pulled in every which way. And a bunch of them looked like they had been there awhile. As the closest Walmart to Yellowstone, this Supercenter had indeed become a destination.

On our first morning in Bozeman, after percolating a pot of coffee and attempting to sweep out some of the hefty layer of western dust BAMF had accumulated, I took a seat up front in order to do some though-the-windshield people watching. Tucked in amongst the behemoth bus-type motor homes, the giant fifth wheel trailers, and the more conservative pop-up campers was a classic Volkswagen Bus. It looked like a bevy of hippies might soon emerge, trailed by clouds of suspicious smoke.

My curiosity piqued, I sipped my coffee and settled in for the show. Before long, a lithe, blonde, dreadlocked woman stepped out, stretched, and fired up an outdoor cook stove. She started a pot of coffee, leaned into the Magic Bus for a quick word with the other yet-to-be-seen occupants, grabbed a tote bag, and headed into the Walmart. I was now fully engaged. My own personal reality TV show, *Bozeman Walmart Parking Lot*.

Out popped a rambunctious, sippy cup–toting, curly-headed toddler, followed quickly by a disheveled young man. Slightly bent and sleepy looking, the poor guy, I reckoned, couldn't wait to get back home to a comfy bed.

Watching their morning routine, my mind wandered back to our family's crazy cross-country Chevy-Van-and-tent trip when The Boy was still in diapers. The extra supplies needed to maintain a traveling toddler took up most of the back of our full-sized van, so I couldn't imagine how these folks were cramming it all into their little bus.

I needed a scheme to get myself a closer look. A book for the little one, that would do it. Grabbing a copy of *Charlotte's Web* I had picked up at a campground trading library, I sauntered over. I was sweetly offered coffee—the only hospitality that the Magic Bus was capable of managing.

"I am pleased you brought a cup. We have no space for extra things. I think of disposing a fourth spoon for some additional space it can make to us," the man half-joked in a lovely German accent. Could this *get* any better?

"I am Hans, my son is Michael, and my wife is Ana. She is back soon."

Little Michael reached up to me, and was soon riding on my hip. He informed me that he was two, then skipped seamlessly from English to German when he addressed his father. What a sweetie.

When Hans proudly gave me the nickel tour, I was floored by the interior. A skilled carpenter, he had transformed his little pop-top hippie wagon into a thing of extremely functional beauty. Rich wood had been fashioned into an elaborate configuration of cabinets, counter space, and sleeping areas. I was blown away. Still, it was damn tight in there, and there was no kitchen or bathroom.

"How long are you on holiday?" I asked. "Are you going to see more National Parks?"

You could have knocked me over with a Montana dust particle when he answered.

"We are to go around the world."

What? I didn't say it aloud, just let my dumbfounded bovine expression carry the conversation.

"We will drive to Pacific Coast and follow south to the end of South America, where we find a boat that accommodates the autobus and go it to New Zealand."

Hans politely gave me a moment to let that all sink in.

I still had some nagging keeping-up-with-the-Joneses feelings when I compared BAMF to some of the half-a-million-dollar showcase mansions-on-wheels we saw on the road—heck, right in that parking lot. There was always someone with a bigger, shinier new toy. But BAMF felt like Graceland compared to the über-pared-down lifestyle of this family. My brain was bouncing between sheer awe and what-the-hell-are-they-thinking. I went with awe.

"Wow. I thought *we* were crazy—you guys are amazing!" I said, giving my still attached-at-the-hip toddler friend a squeeze. "Are you having fun, Michael?"

"Ja!" He replied with a baby-toothed grin. Luckily he used the only German word I knew. Well, besides bier. *That* would have been a weird answer.

When Ana returned, I offered up BAMF's shower to the little family, and to my delight, the offer was enthusiastically accepted. It was the least I could do—when one has such luxurious appointments, one mustn't ever hesitate to share.

These road meetings usually end with a bit of horse trading, and Ana suggested we do some book exchanging. Books, a commodity traded between travelers like prison cigarettes, are well loved, dog-eared, and much coveted. In a world with little storage and even less television, people turn to reading. It warms my soul.

We said our good-byes with hugs, curly-top-of-the-head kisses, and bon voyage wishes, then the Magic Bus putted westward.

Though the past few months had been a joyous, raucous ride, I still found myself obsessing about how people were perceiving me. I've always had trouble with what people thought of me, and motherhood exacerbated the situation. I had to be perceived as the best mom, the best wife, the best at everything. I would pick apart every fault I had, pile it on myself as unforgivable, and light the match. My skills as a housekeeper provided much of the kindling. My mother kept a home so clean you could make soup in the toilet. Never capable of keeping up that level of spotlessness myself, I was always mortified by my dusty baseboards when people stopped by. Seriously. Mortified is not an exaggeration.

I've never looked at the world through eyes that seemed able to see the conventional route as the path forward. The struggle to fit my square-peggliness into society's round hole had caused me much grief, even landing me on the therapist's couch in my thirties. It took a lot of work for me to accept myself as odd, but I've been tentatively letting out the slack on my weird rope ever since. So far, it's been working for me.

So why did I feel one-upped by this couple and their two-year-old? I thought I was being free, true to myself, and a little wild. Now I had to think about driving through South America? Could I ever be the kind of person who has the fearless fortitude to do something like that?

And what about little Michael? What kind of life is in store for him? How many languages will he speak, cultures will be part of his makeup, and ideals will be infused in him before he becomes a man? What will that man be like?

I had learned long ago not to judge others' parenting styles. I've seen some very unconventional moms and dads raise some amazing kids in my time. I will always be the first to speak up on behalf of neglected kids, but short of negligence, I don't give much credence to what society deems the right or wrong way to rear a child.

The Abby Sunderland story comes to mind. Remember Abby? She was the sixteen-year-old sailor who, while attempting to sail her vessel around the world solo, found herself stranded in the middle of the Indian Ocean. Her parents took quite a bit of flack over the situation.

I had looked at that story from many different angles—and, as is usual for me, my feelings were mixed.

The helicopter mommy in me shouted, *What the &#*% were her parents thinking?!* But my empower-your-kids side saw things differently. I too have a child with dangerous dreams: The Boy, who has been flying airplanes since he was thirteen.

Sure, I've heard all the arguments—the most dangerous part of the flight is the drive to the airport . . . blah, blah, blah. Let me tell ya, when it came to plunking my junior high school–aged kid at the helm of a single engine Cessna, I quickly called B.S. on *that* line of logic.

When The Boy came to us with stars in his eyes and told us that he wanted to take flying lessons, my initial reaction was *are you freaking kidding me?* Luckily, David stayed calm and gently peeled me off the ceiling, and we discussed a game plan.

As with all of our kids' endeavors, whether it be violin lessons or rodeo clown school, we required multiple beggings to prove that we were dealing with more than just a passing whim. And beg The Boy did—relentlessly. So we agreed to one free introductory lesson.

Unfortunately, after the flight, The Boy was hooked. In response, we upped the sneaky tactics ante to test his resolve.

I arranged for The Boy to work for a local pilot in exchange for lessons. I was convinced that cleaning planes with kerosene under the vicious Caribbean sun would quickly cure him of his crazy obsession. Nope. In fact, I'd never been more disappointed in one of The Spawn for having so much pride in their work. I'd pick his reeking, sweating, smiling butt up at the airport and hear nothing but excited accounts of airport activities all the way home.

I gave in. Aviation was in his blood. The Boy had found his passion. I couldn't find a fear strong enough, or an argument sound enough, to tear him away from his dream.

My terror didn't ebb as the years went on. I forced David and The Boy into a pact. I was not to hear (or overhear) any talk about these subjects:

—Stall training (also referred to as deadstick—nice, huh?)

—Flying under the hood (yup, wearing a hood over one's head to simulate flying with no visibility)

—Spin training (self-explanatory)

To name just a few of many.

If he was actually going to do this, I needed to be blissfully unaware. And I was—for three years.

The Boy had set the goal of flying his first cross-country solo at the earliest legal age, sixteen. Because we lived in the Virgin Islands, that meant allowing my baby to go up in a plane—all by himself—and fly a hundred miles across the two-mile-deep ocean to Puerto Rico.

The Boy was my only chick left in the nest and, to add to my dismay, his equally horrified sisters began calling home several days before the flight with helpful remarks like:

"Mom, this is crazy,"

and

"Mom, please don't let him do this."

I appreciated their concern, but the last thing I needed was more fear-provoking input.

Heading to the airport, I was a calm-on-the-outside nervous wreck. I was well aware that it wasn't going to do The Boy any good to have a terror-stricken Mommy hovering over him, so I kept a proud-parent brave face. And I did feel real pride in my son as I sat on the sidelines while he fielded questions from newspaper reporters that his equally proud instructor had tipped off. Local Boy Flies Solo on

Sixteenth Birthday. It made good copy. This was, after all, a lofty and rare achievement.

So, like Abby Sunderland's parents, I let him go.

And like Abby Sunderland's parents, I got the scare of a lifetime.

My memory of what happened next is vague—I was so petrified that my brain can't fully recall the details. At the time it was most unhelpful that I had purposefully kept myself ignorant of aviation lingo.

About an hour into the flight I received a phone call from an airport in Puerto Rico. The woman on the other end explained to me that The Boy had never closed his flight plan. They didn't know where he was.

I did what most proactive people do when they can't be proactive—I handed the phone to David and became a comatose blob. I was incapable of comprehending any of the ensuing conversations David engaged in. I just sat there like a petrified lump.

The eternity that seemed to pass while David and The Boy's instructor anxiously sorted out the situation was, in reality, probably only about twenty minutes. Without a doubt the longest twenty minutes of my life.

It turned out to be a simple miscommunication between two airports, then a phone call to the emergency number (ours), rather than the proper contact number (the instructor's) on the flight plan.

Having gone through this experience gave me a glimpse into what Abby Sunderland's parents must have felt when Abby was lost at sea. It's not possible to explain this unique mingling of terror and guilt.

Where is the line between being a parent who supports a child's ambitions and a parent who enables dangerous behavior? I don't have enough information to make a judgment in the case of Abby's parents. I can't know how well Abby trained to make her passage possible, but my guess is seriously and exhaustively, just as The Boy did for his flight.

It is also likely that, like my son, Abby was so focused on her objective that she did not engage in many of the all-too-common behaviors that endanger teens every day. I tally this on the plus side of having a kid with a passion.

Would I allow my own child to sail around the world by herself? Probably not. But then, none of The Spawn are sailors. Abby's parents would probably have reservations about sending Abby up in a plane over the Caribbean all by herself.

The Boy went on to study aviation science in college, pursuing his commercial pilot's license. While I still refuse to listen to the scary stuff, I couldn't be more proud of him. I'm also proud of myself for not letting guilt, fear, and selfishness get in the way of my child's dream.

Now, I wanted to apply that attitude to my own life. Learn to be fearless like Hans, Ana, and Michael, or Abby and The Boy. The latent drive lurking beneath my recovering helicopter mommy exterior was getting my attention. It was time to let it take the driver's seat. I had disentangled myself from a traditional home, job, and way of life, but didn't feel mere disentanglement was the end of it. There was more to come.

I was figuring out who *I* was. The final outcome remained more than a little hazy; after all, what was a helicopter mom without a mission, a SuperMom minus her minivan, a mother sans child?

The time had come to do some serious envelope pushing. To purposefully venture outside of my comfort zone and face my fears in order to become fearless.

Will I be accomplishing the giant feats of my newest friends? Of Abby and The Boy? Perhaps not.

But I knew I was through with baby steps.

23
Fear Conquering and White-Water Rafting

Bozeman, Montana, turned out to be a gem in a number of ways. The little mountain college town had a lot to offer two road-weary Gypsy-Nesters—boundless horizons, lofty peaks, quirky eateries, and a wonderful sense of humor about itself that we couldn't help but relate to.

Honestly, if it weren't for the fact that Bozeman winter temperatures were what they were, we might have considered it a future nesting place.

So maybe we wouldn't be settling in Montana, but I was ready to stay a while. To my surprise, David was on board with the idea too, and not just to prove that he was learning to lighten up on his gotta-get-there mentality. He was feeling a bit of nostalgia being back in the Mountain West and had found all sorts of interesting activities in the surrounding area. He was talking about staying for a week! The wham-bam-thank-you-ma'am travel may not have been all the way out of his system, but at least we were slowing it down.

It was late summer, a glorious season in the Rockies. There was an exciting energy in the air—additionally charged by my (finally) becoming acclimated to the altitude. I began to generate a bit of a wild hair (in addition to the one on my eyelid). The one-upping by the sweet little German family clearly had a stimulating effect on me, and though driving through South America may never be something I would do, I certainly could conquer another one of my many fears in its stead.

The reasons behind the need to conquer those fears had me delving deeper into my psyche during our downtime. I understood why I had become so fearful regarding my children, that had been obvious to me from the day The Piglet was born. Mommies protect their children, period. I may have been a bit over the top in my methods, but I'd be surprised to meet a mother who disagreed with the principle.

However, I didn't stop with the kids. I was also overprotective of myself. While the chicks were still in the nest, risk taking was not an option for me. What would happen to the kids if I did something stupid and died? Or worse, if both David and I died?

When we had date nights, worrying about finding a sitter wasn't worrisome enough for me. I envisioned a drunk broadsiding us in an intersection, a bomb blowing us up in a movie theater, or an E. coli–laced prawn taking us out mafia hit style at a romantic candlelit restaurant. With so much to panic over in the mundane day-to-day, I was not about to take any real gambles in my life.

As time went by, it became easier for me to become complacent with my fearfulness rather than to face it. As much as living in fear sucked, the thought of jumping out of my tightly woven anxiety cocoon created even more internal pandemonium.

While I had children who needed my protection, there was a greater good, a noble cause, a reason for remaining anchored. But the time to break those chains had come. If I continued living in my protective refuge post–child rearing, I'd likely become a quivering shut-in, or possibly a crazy protector of a clowder of cats.

Sifting through Bozeman-area tourist brochures, we stumbled upon a perfect activity to accelerate my transition from fearful to fear-free: white-water rafting down the Gallatin. The very same river that Robert Redford and Brad Pitt waded in while filming *A River Runs Through It*. Perfect—that is, if I eliminated the white-water rafting part.

My trepidation didn't stem from any danger or phobia that most might expect. I love to swim, I love being out on the water, and I am generally fearless when boating. What I was frightfully anxious about was the coldness of the water.

I like my water warm. When I use the word bracing, it is always in a negative context. Never the one to just dive into a pool—no—I use the stairs or a ladder to lower myself inch by careful inch. No use in shocking the goods—a jolt like that could shut down the ol' cardiovascular system.

Obviously, capsizing into an icy Montana river was not my idea of a good time. I was fully convinced that hypothermia could, and would, happen in the dead of summer, especially since the water in the Gallatin had been snow about fifteen minutes prior.

The fact that a helmet was issued as we were outfitted for our excursion didn't faze me much. I understood that the rafting company had to be cautious for insurance reasons—no one wants to play rock-paper-noggin out on the river. I was calm as the three guides—who could only be described as your quintessential dudes—handed out the gear. Surely we wouldn't be doing anything hazardous with these young whipper-snappers at the helm of our vessel.

I happily donned the ray-o'-sunshine yellow helmet, the deliciously dayglow orange vest, and the darling little waterproof booties provided to me. To top off the ensemble I chose a bright blue pair of David's swimming trunks. I was a retina-burning vision of beauty.

Feeling my fashion-forward oats, I boarded the van that would haul us up the canyon to our launching site. During the ride we laughed and kidded with The Dudes. I was now completely convinced that this excursion was going to be a cakewalk—sitting back, dangling my hand in the water while The Dudes paddled me down a lazy river through spectacular scenery.

But things took an abrupt turn toward reality once we reached our destination. The Dudes got all undude-like on us. Uh-oh. Listening to their rapid-fire instructions, I was suddenly made forcefully aware of several things:

1) The river was full of crazy big rocks that must be avoided.

2) I was going to be drenched in freezing cold water, even if I managed to stay in the boat.

3) The darling booties were not for decorative purposes—they were protective gear.

4) I was expected to row (I found this out as a Dude handed me an oar).

5) The reason my garments were so bright was so I could be easily located should I find myself out of the boat, tumbling down the rapids.

I was about to board a blow-up boat with five other people, not one of whom had ever shot a rapid. Our only lifeline was one expert white-water-lovin' Dude. Suddenly I was terrified.

Still, I was on a fear-conquering mission and—by golly—I was goin' in. I held fast to my oar, strode purposefully to the rubber raft, and situated myself on the bench. Our Dude perched himself at the rear, and we were on our way.

Not so rough. The serene beauty of the canyon was mesmerizing. I actually could have dragged my hand along in the water, if the temperature hadn't been so prohibitive. Dude was once again relaxed and dude-like, and we were back to yukking it up.

Then came the first big bend of the river. Like a flume ride at an amusement park (one you could drown on), we were set into serious motion. The floor of the raft quickly took on freezing water. Dude was suddenly shouting out instructions—like a stoned drill sergeant—and we scurried to follow his every command.

The helmet and in-case-of-emergency talk were not just for insurance purposes! We were paddling for our lives—and I was pretty damn sure only one person in our raft had the slightest clue what he was doing. Exhilarating!

There can be a beauty to being scared witless. My mind held only the task at hand. I had completely put my trust in Dude—the same Dude who was bragging on his drinking antics just moments before in the van—because I had no other option. My clueless comrades-in-oars were doing the same. Somehow, under Dude's direction, we became a powerful team of rock-dodging mastodons.

Once we cleared the initial rapids, and the river was peaceful again, cheers of victory went up as oars were double-pumped overhead. Tales of bravado were excitedly tossed around. I felt as though I was aboard a vessel with my only friends in the world. We were a team that, together, conquered a wild river—and our fears. Collectively, we couldn't wait for the next set of rapids, the next challenge ahead.

Bring it on!

24
Balls to the Wall

The next fear to conquer came sooner than we expected and was aimed more at me than Veronica, as Montana had one last surprise for us before we made our way on to the Pacific Northwest. A sign, crazier than any we'd seen since back in the backwoods of the Ozarks, announced the situation:

ROCK CREEK LODGE, CLINTON, MT
TESTICLE FESTIVAL
WORLD FAMOUS FESTIVAL—COME HAVE A BALL

Veronica and I have goaded each other into sampling new, interesting, or even downright weird foods since we met. It's one of our things, and traveling really brings out the daredevil in us. Neither of us can abide backing down from a challenge.

This attitude has led us to some interesting epicurean escapades including seeking the previously mentioned donkey to devour in Sardinia, sampling a guinea pig in Peru, and tasting silkworms in China. These experiences are always accompanied by laughter, camaraderie, and a deep immersion into a local lifestyle. It's tough to beat.

Now it was Montana's turn to join the ranks of our questionable culinary challenges. Having spent most of my childhood summers in the Rocky Mountains, I had heard the lore of the alpine oyster, but never had the balls to try one. That was about to change. Veronica already had that I-dare-you grin spreading across her face.

At the next exit, Clinton appeared to consist of one lonesome rundown building that was quite possibly abandoned. But in the wide-open spaces of Montana, a gathering of two or more people can qualify as a town.

"Should we check it out?" I asked, knowing there was no way we were going to miss this.

Without waiting for an answer, I took the exit. All of a sudden it felt like we were traveling through another dimension. A dimension not only of sight and sound, but of mind. A journey into a wondrous land whose boundaries are that of imagination, deep fryers, Idaho, and Canada. Wait, there's a signpost up ahead, our next stop: The Testicle Zone!

But as we pulled into the lot of the seemingly uninhabited building, another sign informed us that we had missed the notorious Testy Festy by a couple of weeks. Probably a good thing since, from the looks of the place, a biker New Year's Eve party would've been tame by comparison. Even after a fortnight, evidence of the carnage was notably apparent. A dilapidated, falling-down stage, trash and beverage bottles strewn about, muddy ruts every which way, and a few banners clinging askew to the walls were a testament to the testicular bash.

However, luck was on our side that day. The roadhouse was not vacant. There were inhabitants in the Rock Creek Lodge, and they did not need a special occasion to have a ball serving up Rocky Mountain oysters, a.k.a. cowboy caviar, prairie oysters, or Montana tendergroin. They are the special every day.

I was pretty sure Veronica was only vaguely familiar with the concept of Rocky Mountain oysters, and might not fully grasp what we were about to consume, so I asked, "Do you know what we're doing?"

"I think I caught the drift from the signs and stuff."

She had seen several images of cartoon bulls with pained expressions, clutching their crotches where some glands used to be hanging around. Wait, is it possible to clutch with hooves?

"And from the looks of them, I guess they're using, um, you know, cows?"

"Generally a bull would be necessary, honey, but I always thought they snipped sheep back in Colorado."

Just thinking about the procedure had started a process down in my nether regions that involved certain parts of my anatomy retracting like the landing gear on a jumbo jet. Then it hit me—Veronica *knew* what was happening. She was very aware that this particular gastronomic undertaking was going to be much harder on me than her.

"Wipe that grin off your face—just for that, you have to go first."

We ordered at the bar, figuring several ice-cold malt beverages might be needed to wash down our snack, and were informed by the bartender that the Rock Creek Lodge testicles are indeed from unlucky bulls, are thinly sliced, breaded, spiced, deep-fried, and served with a zesty cocktail sauce.

"Try not to think about it and just pop 'em down," he advised.

So we did. Contrary to what everyone always says, Rocky Mountain oysters do not taste anything like chicken—or oysters for that matter. Actually, all we could taste was highly spiced batter supersaturated in as much grease and cocktail sauce as it could hold. Just as well.

We did our best, but there was no way we were finishing what was in that basket. I was greatly relieved when they were removed from our presence. Seeing my relief, Veronica upped the ante by asking the bartender for a peek at a precooked, presliced testicle. He burst out laughing. We weren't the first to make this request, and he was more than happy to oblige.

"Follow me." He nodded, heading into the kitchen.

Next thing I knew we were face-to-face with a frozen football-sized, vein-riddled monstrosity. When Veronica asked how it was primed for slicing, I knew I had to leave. As I headed for the bathroom, their discussion trailed off out of my hearing range.

". . . then it's defrosted, and this skin here has to be peeled back. After that we can take a knife . . ."

Trust me, talk like that can make a man jittery.

* * * * *

Sampling local delicacies gives us another layer of understanding when exploring a new neck of the woods. It's a great way to experience the idiosyncrasies of an area and its culture. These peculiarities usually have roots dating back centuries, and stem from rituals and mores that serve to define a people.

Recipes and dishes get passed down for generations and reflect traditions that have become an integral part of the society. These often have stories that have been woven into the fabric of family celebrations, religious observances, and holiday gatherings, and help make a region stand out from the surrounding areas.

The ingredients usually have a tale to tell too, whether from long-held practice or newfound availability, that provides a perspective into the history of a population.

For example, Acadians didn't eat crawfish before they were run out of Canada 250 years ago, but when they settled in south Louisiana and became known as Cajuns, the prevalence of the little mudbugs made them a staple.

Sadly, a great deal of this diversity is being homogenized out of our modern lives. We live in a world where we are never very far from the nearest mass-produced, paper-wrapped hamburger, but all in all, I'd rather eat Sardinian ass. Just because something seems strange to us doesn't mean it can't be delicious.

We certainly found that to be true of the bone marrow pudding with tongue in cheek marmalade we had in San Antonio, or fiery hot quahog beachside in Rhode Island, or turtle soup in New Orleans.

What may strike a visitor as odd is perfectly normal to the locals, like those crawdads in Louisiana, poutine in Canada, or fatballs in Holland—Michigan, that is. Yes, we consumed something called a fatball.

After we arrived in Generic Midwestern College Town, we took a little side trip to the town of Holland for their Tulip Time festival. Walking through the displays and vendors of the flower fest, we came upon a huge line at one of the food stands and had to check it out. What on earth could be so popular? The sign said it all:

OLDE WORLD DELI FATBALLS

What in the hell? We had to try one—after all, they're both "Olde World" and "Deli."

Known by many names back in the old country, *oliebollen, vet ballen, smoutebollen,* or *oliekoecken,* these Dutch treats are grapefruit-sized globs of deep-fried dough (in this case sharing a deep fryer with corn dogs and french fries), split open, slathered with pie filling, and served in an oil-absorbing paper cone. Now that's good eatin'.

This is no light snack. They are closer in density to a dumbbell than a doughnut. Devouring a fatball can give the biceps, as well as some more central parts of the anatomy, a workout.

Personally, I think they should be called fat bombs, because they lay like a land mine in the stomach. But as far as our experience of greasy gut explosive devices goes, the fatball falls well short of the ultimate weapon of mass (in)digestion.

That distinction would have to go to the Triple D Burger at Joe's Gizzard City. The Triple D is a huge patty of ground cow, topped with onions, pickles, tomatoes, and American cheese, dipped in batter and deep-fried, bun and all.

If that terrifying tower isn't quite enough of a belly bunker buster, the fine chefs at Gizzard City will be happy to batter up and toss into boiling oil anything from appetizers like chicken gizzards, meatballs, pickles, or olives to desserts like cheesecake, Oreos, ice cream, or Twinkies. A MASH unit is on standby outside.

* * * * *

Once we put Montana in our rearview mirror and ventured into the Pacific Northwest, the salmon were running upstream in their insane, unstoppable quest to spawn. The horniest teenager ever to have a hormone surge is but a timid prude compared to these naiant sex fiends. This fortunate timing meant that two of our favorite things could coalesce: seafood and festivals.

In the Seattle suburb of Issaquah, thousands of cohos and chinooks were fighting their way up Issaquah Creek, desperate to return to the Washington State Fish Hatchery from whence they came. This fascinating annual phenomenon has spawned the beloved Salmon Fest. As fests go, this is a big one. For forty years, hundreds of thousands of people have come to celebrate the return of the salmon. Scores of artists hawking their wares, five stages with all-day music, and dozens of food vendors make for a good time for all.

But in an odd quirk, almost none of the available vittles contained any salmon whatsoever. Where were all the salmon steaks, sandwiches, salads, and sushi? Not here. All we could find was one booth selling packaged smoked salmon and a couple of cubicles with questionable fried cakes.

We were hoping for better luck at the Dungeness Crab & Seafood Festival in Port Angeles, on the northern coast of Washington. Nestled between the Olympic Mountains and the Strait of Juan de Fuca, scenic beauty and ginormous trees define this area. We felt confident that this was the place to be for any decapod-desiring seafood lover.

Crab Fest turned out to be a bit of a pipsqueak compared to Salmon Fest, but what it lacked in size, it more than made up for in crustacean crackin' tastiness. We even got the chance to catch our own grub, trying our hands at crabbing in the Grab-a-Crab Derby on the pier. For twelve dollars we were handed a little contraption with snares made from loops of fishing line, and pointed toward an oversized tank full of crabs. The promise that they'd cook up our catch was included in the bargain.

If it had been left up to me, we would have starved. I couldn't snag one of the claw-footed buggers to save my life, but Veronica snatched them out of the water like an old salt. She snared six of them, squealing with delight each time.

After choosing the tastiest-looking two for the steamer, we released the others back into the wilds of the tank. Our fresh Dungeness dinner was served up with corn, coleslaw, music, and beer. What's not to like? Plus, there's nothing more satisfying than enjoying a meal you caught yourself. Or that your wife caught for you.

25
50 @ 50

While we were in Washington, I couldn't help but think about the major milestone waiting for me below the border. I did my best to conceal my giddy excitement, but I was more than ready to head south and mark off my fiftieth state, Oregon.

This seemed like a pretty big achievement to me, so I set out to do a little investigating. Just how rare is it for a person to have set foot in all fifty states?

According to the websites that came up when I searched "visit all fifty states," many people would like to do it, and quite a few have succeeded. I found out that Richard Nixon was the first president to travel to all fifty states. Several since then, including our current commander in chief, have also accomplished the feat.

Digging deeper, I discovered several stories about individuals trying to make it more challenging by introducing quirky twists. On a motorcycle, all in one year, while backpacking, or all by themselves. I personally would give huge laurels to the first person to do it alphabetically. Now that would be a feat. Just making the Alabama–Alaska–Arizona and Georgia–Hawaii–Idaho jumps without touching any states in between should seal a spot in the travel hall of fame.

But the Internet in all its omnipotent glory could not seem to provide me with a credible figure as to how many people have actually managed to make it to every state. How extraordinary was I about to become?

Asking the cyber swami, "What percentage of Americans have been to all 50 states?" produced a couple of answers, with absolutely no references, that I'm pretty sure were way off.

One site said 37 percent—no way—another had 9 percent, which still seemed a little high and had no corroboration whatsoever. Yet another said 14 percent, but also claimed that Texas is the largest state in the union, making me more than a tad suspicious of its accuracy.

I continued my investigation by attempting several variations of my inquiry. But try as I might, I simply could not find an exit off the information superhighway that had a definitive answer. Ten percent of Americans? I think not. Five? Maybe. One percent? More? Less? I don't know, and the data didn't seem to be available.

It's not often that the World Wide Web doesn't have an answer, so I took that to mean it's a fairly rare feat indeed. Makes a guy feel kinda special.

Following Highway 101 down the coast—with the wiper blades clearing the spray of the Pacific Ocean surf off the windshield—we saw the Columbia River bridge, connecting Washington with the final star on my flag. The bridge is a massive structure of nearly four miles, spanning the broad waterway where Lewis and Clark completed their westward expedition. A fitting border crossing to usher in my stint as a Fifty Stater, I thought.

Once we cleared the bridge, and rolled onto terra firma in Oregon, Veronica asked if I wanted to kiss the ground. I didn't really feel compelled to pull a Pope's arrival imitation, even though I was duly proud of my accomplishment.

I had visited all fifty states. And it only took me fifty years. That's right, my quest had been completed in the same year that I turned the calendar from my forty-ninth to my fiftieth year.

With that goal realized, we turned our attention back to the original concept for our journey. Veronica had several segments of extended family down in Southern California, her childhood home, that we hadn't seen in ages. We were on a mission to work our way down there in time to spend Thanksgiving with the lot of them. As an added bonus, the route we had chosen would take us through the Redwoods, Yosemite, and Big Sur.

We had seen some pretty freakin' big trees along the coasts of Washington and Oregon, but nothing like what we were seeing as we entered

California. We knew we must be getting close to the Redwoods, but weren't very sure where they officially started or where the best groves might be. We assumed (and everyone knows what happens when you do that) that the biggest and best redwoods would be in Redwoods National Park, a couple of hours' drive to the south. Wrong. Because of their late entry into the save-the-redwoods movement, the National Park Service comes up short to several California State Parks in the preserving big, fat, tall trees department.

One of the best of those state-run preserves is Jedediah Smith State Park, a place we fortuitously stumbled upon simply because it was getting late and we needed a place to park BAMF for the night. What a parking spot we found! We tucked our weary little rolling house between two towering trees with trunks the size of Donald Trump's ego.

In the morning we wandered through the forest in complete awe of some of nature's largest and oldest living things. Pretty soon their phenomenal size had our perspective turned all askew, and we began to feel like we were in an alien world.

It turns out that in a way we were. We were hiking through the area in which the *Star Wars Return of the Jedi* chase scene on the flying motorbike speeder thingies was filmed, and felt transported to the Forest Moon of the planet Endor, home to those adorable little teddy bear tough guys, the Ewoks. Pretty groovy, and a blast to talk about while gawking up at the surreal trees.

Back on Earth, we drove and walked through stand after stand of the world's most monumental trees and noticed two things happening to us. Our necks were killing us from constantly looking up while straining to see the tops of the behemoths, and we began to feel miniature.

So we felt like giants once we left the Redwoods and drove through forests of normal, everyday, run-of-the-mill big trees. But soon enough the ginormous mountain peaks and sheer cliffs of Yosemite had us feeling like pipsqueaks again.

Like most of our generation, we first heard of Yosemite from *Looney Tunes*. On childhood Saturday mornings Yosemite Sam bellerin'

"Reach fer the sky, fragnabbit!" introduced us to the name, but he had nothing to do with the venerable National Park. *Looney Tunes* director Friz Freleng just liked the plumb Western sound of California's premier park for his sourdough, loudmouthed, going-off-all-half-cocked, six-shootin' little fella. A couple thousand Saturday mornings later, yer flea-bitten, GypsyNestin' varmints finally met up with Sam's namesake as we entered the park from the west, and the iconic valley spread out before us in a dazzling panorama.

Ancient glaciers carved the Yosemite Valley nearly half a mile deep, leaving behind stark rock faces that climbers flock to for the ultimate challenge. There would be no cliff climbing for us though; we draw the fear conquering line well below two thousand feet of vertical granite. Instead we spent our day on the valley floor hiking and biking to waterfalls and magnificent vistas.

We made it back to our campsite just in time to watch a full moon rise over the Half Dome mountain. Later, basking in the moonglow and campfire, we heard something stirring in the woods. What could it be? It was Halloween, so maybe ghosts? Goblins? Sam? It was certainly something that goes bump in the night.

The lunar lumination revealed a large, black furry creature lumbering through the camps. Whatever it was it must have been hungry, because it nearly took out the tent on the next site over from us, then headed right past us and straight toward a large group enjoying a late dinner.

Just when we were thinking *best costume ever*, the moonlight and trail of nostril-searing odor exuding from the beast opened our eyes. Great gallopin' horny-toads! That ornery fur-bearin' critter must be one of them thar bears we'd constantly been warned about throughout the park. Confound it, they're genuine, and more than a bit scary in real life.

The alarm went out. A mob of campers formed and began banging on pots and pans while shouting and waving torches (that's Brit for flashlights in this case). Jumping up to join the pack and add our lanterns to the posse, we drove the creature from our midst. It felt like the villagers in a cheesy old Frankenstein flick scaring the poor monster back into his lair. Happy Halloween.

In the safety of the morning light, and with November upon us, the time had come to continue south so as to partake of the Thanksgiving feast with Veronica's kinfolk. We swung back over to the coast and moseyed along the scenic route.

The Pacific Coast Highway, through the central part of California known as Big Sur, is one remarkable stretch of road. It skirts along where the mountains meet the sea, with thirty-three bridges connecting one wickedly winding section of cliff-clinging roadway to the next. Often the landscape drops directly off from the edge of the roadside to the water hundreds of feet down.

Fully aware of how crucial it was to keep the old eyeballs glued to the blacktop, or else wind up in the ocean below, I did my best to ignore the scenic viewing opportunities off to either side.

More than once Veronica had to give me gentle reminders that certain death awaited if I didn't focus. Okay, some not so gentle, depending on how many wheels were hanging over the side at any given moment. But we survived and made it down to Southern California in one piece, and in plenty of time for the impending holiday.

26
No Home for the Holidays

Thanksgiving has long been my favorite holiday. I love it all, the smell of the turkey in the oven, the din of football on the tube, the snacking on the obligatory relish tray, sneaking bites of searing-hot stuffing from the bird along the way, and the semi-disgusting *thwauuuuuck* sucking sound of the cranberry sauce coming out of the can that unmistakably signals it's chow time.

We have, like most every family, fine-tuned our menu over the years. It evolved into a perfect starch-laden masterpiece consisting of Veronica's mother's stuffing, my mother's twice-baked potatoes, mashed potatoes, sweet potatoes, crescent rolls, pumpkin pie, and of course, the turkey. For years we tried to introduce something green into the mix. Whether it was peas, broccoli, salad, zucchini, or even the classic green bean casserole, inevitably it would sit untouched upon the table. We quit trying.

Even as the chicks moved away, and short college breaks combined with long travel distances wouldn't allow them to make it home for the holiday, we continued to lay out the same spread for our dwindling brood. But here we were with no brood at all, and no home either. It was enough to make me a little blue, and would probably have put my resident recovering helicopter mommy into a full-blown empty nest funk, if not for a perfect diversion.

Veronica hadn't seen her brother Jeff since their mother's funeral more than a decade prior. The multitude of miles that separate St. Croix from Southern California, plus kids and jobs, both his and ours, had pushed getting together into the realm of got to find a way to do it sometime soon. Sometime soon turned into years and years, so her excitement at their reunion trumped any melancholy feelings she may have been experiencing.

Veronica's family has always amazed me. Coming from a traditional heartland upbringing, with Mom and Dad still together after nearly sixty years, a boatload of siblings, time-honored traditions, and guarded conventional appearances, I'm always genuinely astounded by the free-form concept of family that Veronica and her California clan practice. Cross-country moves, divorce, remarriage, and even deaths have not lessened the love that this tribe has for one another. This year they were all meeting up for a huge holiday family reunion, and we happened to be just in time.

This would be the mother of all Thanksgivings, over forty people, hosted by Veronica's ex-step-sister-in-law, Tinker. Tinker is the wife of Veronica's stepfather's oldest child from the wife before Veronica's mom . . . never mind, Veronica just calls Tinker her sister. Anyway, Veronica would be seeing all of her stepsiblings, many of whom now have families of their own, plus her brother's family and stepfather's new wife for the first time in over a decade. Some for the first time ever.

I was impressed. The congregation of relations, steprelations, in-laws, and exes sounded like a recipe for disaster to me, but it was nothing of the sort. Each relative, no matter how distant, was treated like the closest of kin.

It was brilliant how smoothly Veronica could breeze through a complex family connection for an introduction. Here's how she presented herself to an ex-step-niece's new boyfriend:

"Okay, you know Julie over there. Julie is your girlfriend's grandma and Rowland's first wife. You also know Barbara here. Barbara is Rowland's beautiful new bride. Then Maryann, who died ten years ago in Rowland's arms, was Rowland's second wife and my mom."

The boyfriend didn't even blink, and with a nice-to-meet-you hug he was officially part of the family.

The old don't talk with your mouth full rule was certainly suspended for the day. Everyone got filled in while filling up on the time-honored, potluck-style holiday offerings, including my mom's twice-baked potatoes that we brought, just in case the starch content of the feast fell below 90 percent. We couldn't have asked for a better first empty nest Thanksgiving.

The only lumps in the gravy—and our throats—came when the kids called to wish us what has become our customary family greeting for the holiday, "Happy Thanksgiving, Butthole!"

This must be delivered in a preposterously exaggerated Southern accent to be properly festive. Perhaps I should explain.

Many moons ago, back in Nashville, we took the young 'uns to the grocery store on the day before Thanksgiving for some last-minute starch reinforcements. Decibel was certain we needed a fourth tube of crescent rolls. Our quest was interrupted by a high-volume verbal altercation in the frozen food aisle. As the conflict escalated, every single shopper in the store became fully aware that this couple, who put the red in redneck, were not in full agreement as to what should be served for dessert at their holiday meal. I figured I'd been around the block a time or two, but I never heard adjectives like those used to describe pies before. Never will again, I hope. Plus, I'm pretty sure a bunch of those words aren't even supposed to be used as adjectives.

Then the *real* airing of the grievances began in, shall we say, even more colorful language, and at a volume that ensured everyone all the way into the parking lot could share the holiday joy of being included in this feud. Methinks there may have been a tiny bit more behind the fracas than just picking between apple- or pumpkin-filled baked goods.

Since Veronica and I only had four hands to cover six innocent little ears, we made a mad dash for the checkout line. Our getaway didn't pan out as planned though. The ever demure Mrs. R. Neck got fed up and catapulted her shopping cart, filled with unacceptable sweets, toward the love of her life, then stormed past us for the exit. Before stepping out, she delivered this classic top-of-the-lungs, take-that-you-bastard parting shot:

"Happy Thanksgiving, Butthole!"

A tradition was born.

By the end of our phone conversations, all three kids had asked, "Where are we going to have Christmas?"

The dilemma was reminiscent of Christmases past. When we first had children the holidays posed a problem for us, one no doubt most new parents face. Whose family would we visit? Both sides wanted to spoil their grandchildren and have a big family holiday, but none of the grandparents lived nearby, or near each other. We worked it out by explaining that we wanted to create our own Christmas traditions with our kids, in our own home. If extended family wanted to see us, they were more than welcome to come and join in. A few times they did, and a few times we traveled, but mostly we spent our yuletides at home, just the five of us.

This year we would not be home. The stockings would not be hung on BAMF's tailpipe with care.

Luckily, we have discovered that it really doesn't matter where we are, or what's on the table. Having a happy holiday is all about being together. One of our best family memories involved an ill-fated trip to Cleveland for a great-grandpa visit. All-day driving left us stuck in a hotel with three teenagers on Thanksgiving night, and not an open restaurant to be found. So we made a spread on the bed of tortilla chips and beef jerky from the mini mart next door. They didn't have any pies, but we managed to hold our tongues, other than the requisite "Happy Thanksgiving" anatomical greetings, and have an unconventional holiday feast. One that all five of us look back on with fond feelings.

Warm memory or not, the girls were determined to avoid a replay, so they agreed to host Christmas in their New York City apartments. They even set it up for The Boy to fly in after his semester finals.

The only snag for us was distance. There was no way we were deadhead driving coast to coast. But Jeff was kind enough to offer his driveway as a BAMF parking spot, so off we flew to the Big Apple for our first empty nest Noel.

* * * * *

New York City is freaking magical at Christmastime. They really deck them halls. David and I went into full tourist mode and visited all of the famous holiday hot spots. We caught the bigger-than-expected Rockefeller Center Christmas tree and the surprisingly itty-bitty skating rink at the bottom of it, the lights along Fifth Avenue, and the Macy's on Thirty-Fourth Street with the enchanting window displays and most perfect Santa ever. He's the real one—we've seen proof of it in a movie. Even the Central Park carriages were all dolled up, but we couldn't convince a single driver to put antlers or a red nose on his horse. That would've been wicked sweet.

After a few days of running around like maniacs, taking in all the city had to offer, we did slow down for the big day. We made a huge meal in The Piglet's teeny studio apartment. With a miniature tree sparkling, the hide-a-bed festively extended for extra seating, Nat King Cole playing on the iPod, and the fireplace channel crackling on TV, we had our Christmas. Probably not a new tradition—the kids will no doubt form their own as the years go by—but it was just fine for our inaugural homeless holiday season.

Admittedly, it was quite a departure from previous years, but I have to say, it was *much* easier on me, stresswise.

I no longer had to find forgot-where-I-hid-them presents, then hurriedly wrap them while barricaded in a closet with a flashlight in my teeth and covered in packing tape. There was no racing from Christmas pageant to winter recital to endless Nutcracker rehearsals. Gone was the digging out of the boxes from the attic, the untangling of the strings of lights, and the setting up of the fake tree (real ones always ended up making us sad when they turned brown and we had to take them down around Valentine's Day).

The best part of our first empty nest Christmas was the excitement on our kids' faces as they gave gifts to one another. The love they shared and the happiness they wanted to give one another is what made the Most Wonderful Time of the Year, well, the most wonderful time of the year.

I sat back with a Cheshire cat grin on my face watching them relate to one another as young adults. The Piglet, who was five when The Boy was born, quickly reverted to her vice-Mommy persona. She still gets miffed if The Boy comes up with an opinion that differs from hers. She feels she has raised him better than that. Nothing less than pure adoration from him shall be tolerated.

They all have a tendency to revert back to being wild-eyed children when they get together. In no time at all Decibel and The Boy began bickering and poking each other. Before long The Piglet jumped in too. It felt like they were squabbling in an attempt to keep their childhoods alive. Being with Mom and Dad gave them a chance to escape the responsibilities of their new adult lives for a few days. Who was I to burst that bubble?

Then I heard the inevitable. "Mooooooooom! Tell The Boy to stop it!"

I turned around with a huge grin on my face, "Don't *make* me come over there!"

I was in heaven. I couldn't care less about any other presents, just give me mommy duty again.

27
Grandchildish Behavior

The night before we flew back to the West Coast, The Piglet and Decibel hit me with an unexpected going-away present.

"All of our friends' mothers are on crazy grandma patrol. How come you aren't nagging us about having babies?"

Seriously? I was fairly certain that they were just looking for an opening to inflict a little farewell jab. But during the course of the discourse I got the feeling that they might be getting miffed by my lack of interest. Even though I knew—good *and* well—that neither of the girls was even remotely at a procreating place in life. In fact, one of them says she finds the birthing process so totally repulsive that she wants to be "knocked out like the good old days" should the event ever occur.

But I hadn't really pondered the subject before, except in the abstract, so just the asking of the question got me thinking.

If I were to have a grandbaby, I think I would be the best grandma ever. That child would be the most loved and cherished little one on the face of the earth. I think David would be even nuttier; he's crazy about kids, and kids love him right back. It would be a battle just to pry the tot off of his aching horsey-ridden back.

But, if I never have grandkids, that's all right, too. I'm not one of those passing-along-the-genes/carrying-on-the-family-name kinda gals. There's no inherent longing in my breast—I actually view that stuff as sort of archaic. Maybe this is a backlash from the incessant hints my mother-in-law dropped as soon as David and I got hitched.

In her defense, David is the fourth of five children, and was the first to marry—she had waited a *long* time by then. All of her girlfriends were winning the Grandma Game back in a time when that baby tally really meant something.

Baby begging doesn't seem to be as much a part of our generation's psyche, but grandma pride seems to have survived in full force. Facebook has opened my eyes to that. Once one of my friends becomes a grandparent, their profile becomes a never-ending barrage of baby pictures. They're worse than the new mothers. I understand it though, and I'll probably be a photo-posting maniac myself should the time ever come.

To be honest, one of the reasons for my lack of longing is unabashed selfishness. I like having my kids all to myself when we visit. No husbands, wives, or diaper changes to disrupt my time with them. I feel I'm just getting to know them as adults, and I am loving the process. I don't want to share.

Genetics may play into my thinking as well. My mother-in-law, as one might imagine, was truly excited when I announced my first upcoming bundle of joy. My side of the family reacted a bit differently. My mother was properly excited, but you would have thought I purposefully dropped an anvil on my dad. He was dismayed. He had to know that I was at an age where this type of thing could happen, he just couldn't believe that *he* was.

"I'm too young to be a grandfather!"

Like my goal had been to put the final nail in the coffin of his fading youth. Grandfatherdom seemed to be a direct affront to the vernal image he had of himself.

As taken aback as I was at the time, I have to admit that I get it today. Personality is something I've inherited from my dad, and—honestly—the idea of me being a grandma stings a bit.

I also wonder how influenced by outside factors I might be. In our society, we are past the point where we need to quickly pump out babies to help out on the farm, carry on the family name, or populate the Wild West. There are an awful lot of people on this little planet of ours, and I have to say I'm glad we're slowing down with the baby birthing bit.

Prior to my generation, most women sought status in marrying well, having children, and keeping a nice home. Even if it took a secret stash of Valium to keep many of them on the "meet hubby at the door in pumps and pearls holding a martini" track. Ladies were faced with an either/or proposition; marriage and kids, or be an old maid with a career. Society hardly embraced women who did things on their own, and mixing parenthood and profession was barely an option.

During the course of my childbearing years, modern womanhood was faced with new realities. Our mothers expected us to marry young and start a family, as was customary in their day. Some of us did, many did not. For most though, married, single, parent or not, working became a more widely accepted route. This created a divide that grew wider as the years passed. Before we knew what hit us, women were being denounced for *not* entering the workforce and opting to stay at home.

In the midst of this reversal, we women could be our own worst enemies. Having had friends in both camps, I heard the rumblings, "What does she *do* all day long sitting at home with kids? That would drive me crazy," or, "Bless her heart, she just doesn't understand how fulfilling motherhood is," or, the worst, "Those poor kids, their mother cares more about her job than she cares about them." We had more choices, and with those choices came a multitude of opinions.

Modern young women like my daughters are of a different mindset than their predecessors. They've evolved into what I believe many women of my generation were hoping for themselves. At least in New York City, society freely allows them to be single until they decide not to be. Their status doesn't rise or fall on the decision to marry or have children. They won't be called old maids. They can be working women without being labeled "working women." I'm fairly certain that they are blissfully unaware of the cruel connotation that lovely little double entendre used to carry.

I feel pride and awe when I observe my daughters and their friends in their natural habitat. They are comfortable in their own skins in a way I've never been. They conquer their fears head-on—and the world they live in allows it. If folks disapprove, they don't give a damn. It's beautiful to watch.

The Spawn will set their reproductive itinerary at their own pace. It is not something I need to stick my pointy nose into. The potential for disaster looms large if a person is nagged into breeding before they are prepared, whether by a parent, society, or even a spouse. If one of our babies feels the time is right to reproduce, I'll be right there with helpful hints on nausea, mood swings, vomit stain elimination, and the like.

Until then, I'll be glad to have them all to myself.

* * * * *

I slipped into the kitchen to steer clear of the whole mother-daughter grandchildren conversation. It's just none of my business. If they want advice on almost any subject, I am more than happy to blather on at great length, leaving no option unexplored in a valiant effort to impart my vast repository of wisdom and experience to my beloved offspring. But their personal lives? I am not about to dive into that pool.

Honestly, I was also afraid I might incriminate myself by admitting that I would love to have grandchildren. I am drool-resistant, I attract dirt, I love to wallow, and I don't mind eating things off of the ground. Oh, and sometimes I need changing. We would be peas in a pod. No wonder Veronica doesn't feel a strong need for a grandbaby. When the girls brought it up she should have just said, "Who needs grandchildren? I've got your father."

So when, or I guess if, our grandparenting time comes, I'll fit right in with the next generation. That's not to say that I would ever push our kids toward procreation; I am a firm believer in letting our adult children live their own lives. But I will be one ecstatic pappy should the time ever come.

I can't help thinking how fun it would be to have some new little rug rats running 'round. Sofa cushion forts to be constructed, trashcan lid sled races to run, rockets to launch, and old lawnmower/tricycle/roller-skate/beanbag-chair vehicles to be made. Maybe even a mad, mud-filled attempt at tunneling under the neighbor's house. Oh wait, that was my childhood. So what, we can relive it all with nothing more than a sack lunch and a big idea.

And there is that one huge advantage to grandchildren, the icing on the face—I mean, cake. They go home at some point. Then Veronica and I can go on with our GypsyNesting lives. All of the fun without all that pesky responsibility. Even better, since we've sold the nest, when the grape juice–filled sippy cup does a slo-mo two-and-a-half gainer with a lid-releasing twist across the room, we will be spectators from the visiting team. I'll give it an 8.5 with wild applause. We will be able to truly appreciate the talents of our progeny.

That peanut butter and jelly face print on the hall closet door? Nice likeness.

The terrarium complete with amphibian wildlife in the bathtub? Educational.

The chemistry/cooking experiment involving chocolate pudding, Cheerios, a two-liter bottle of Diet Pepsi, bag of frozen peas, and the blender? Nourishing, and builds character.

As long as I don't actually join in on the mess making, and it will be extremely difficult not to, it won't be my problem. I'll offer to help clean up, but I don't have to.

Grandchildren will also provide the final piece in the puzzle for a complete education for our kids. No child ever really knows what their parents went through until they have children of their own. No, I'm not wishing the old "I hope you have a kid just like you someday" re-venge on them. Actually, maybe I should. I hope they are so lucky as to have great kids like themselves. I'm just saying that parenthood is, without a doubt, the world's biggest learning experience.

So I definitely look forward to the day when I can roll all over the living room floor with my kids' kids. I will boldly face the possibility of projectile vomit all over my shirt, gum-based food products in my hair, melted mystery candy-like substances in my pockets, and the inevitable stained knees, buttocks, elbows, and everywhere else on my clothes. I was a willing target for it in my daddy days, and it's nothing a little Tide and a washing machine can't handle.

My aching back might be a different story.

28
Withdrawal

I hardly said a word to David on the transcontinental flight back to California. All I wanted to do was sleep, and he seemed to be thinking pretty hard about something anyway. I couldn't shake the blues, the feeling of emptiness.

Stuck in that in-between state of sleep and wakefulness that only plane travel can provide, my brain toggled from past to present.

I drifted back to when The Piglet was first taking wing. We decided that David should escort her to college while I stayed home to tend the nest. At the airport, I tagged along up to the security line, bravely smiled and waved as they put their shoes back on and headed for the gate, and then sat in my car in the parking lot and cried like Tammy Faye Bakker on the second day of her period. It was a regular air-sucking, mascara-dripping, please-God-nobody-see-me sob fest. Not my finest moment.

Back at home with Decibel and The Boy, I was thankfully able to focus my helicopter mom hovering on their activities. It was a darn good thing they were there, because otherwise I might have followed The Piglet to college.

Then a movie-like montage of our blissful visit to New York began to play under my pretending-to-be-sleeping eyelids. That first take-your-breath-away gasp I uttered when I saw each of my children for the first time in months. My God, they're beautiful. The goofy antics on the subway whilst surrounded by disinterested New Yorkers. The laughing 'til someone publicly spit-takes a sip of red wine, something I'm only capable of doing with Decibel and The Piglet. I had replays of our spirited debates that continue a family tradition. Last-minute Christmas shopping in techno-music-blaring clothing stores with monosyllabic names like Pink, Funk, Dream, and Wear. The mobs of people, the honking, the sirens, the screeching of trains. Come to think of it, New York is really, really loud.

Otherwise I might be actively lobbying to move to the city to be close to The Piglet and Decibel. The Boy could tag along once he finished college. We could be one big happy family again. I could fire back up the chopper, be overbearing, and butt my nose back into their new adult lives. They'd love it. Right. Good thing the never-ending racket of NYC is so prohibitive.

There's nowhere to escape the constant bombardment of sound. The shops and restaurants often have doors open to the street noise, or music blaring, or both. The commotion even permeates apartment walls, and fuggedaboutit if the windows are open. If I were to live in Manhattan, I'd need a penthouse apartment in a skyscraper just to get some peace. I can't imagine being able to afford *that* anytime soon.

Maybe we're used to the relative quiet of our BAMF-dwelling existence, or maybe the old ears ain't what they used to be, but I don't know how anyone can carry on a conversation in the city. Lord knows, nothing makes a lady feel young like having to cup her hand behind her ear and yell *what?!* a million times with a hoarse, overused voice. Yet, out of the bedlam came inspiration.

In one of our family's favorite eateries, called Bread—in keeping with the city's monosyllabic rule—I came up with an idea for New York's newest hot spot. However, even though Bread is laid back by NYC standards, between the full-frontal volume of the background music and the rising level of the patrons' conversations competing against it, I couldn't muster up enough voice to share my big idea with the entire table. So I decided to relay it to the closest person.

I nudged David and said, "Wouldn't it be great if there were a place we could go where we could all hear each other?"

"*What?!*"

He was sitting right beside me, but years of standing next to drummers had taken a toll.

I was about to reattempt when Decibel, whose voice easily cut through the din, informed me that, "*Mom*, you're yelling again."

David was looking at me inquisitively. I could see he was shifting into lip reading mode, so I tried again.

"Wouldn't it be great if there was some place we could go where we could all hear each other?"

"You hate that home plate we should go to be near beach otters?"

He sucks at reading lips.

"No, I have a great idea for a night club." I nearly shouted while trying to form my words visually and obviously.

"You need some Vicks VapoRub?"

"Your lip reading is very impressive."

"You keep heating cherry espresso?"

"Never mind, I'll tell you outside."

"You want to see *The Princess Bride*?"

I gave up and went back to my soup. He took the cue and happily resumed consumption too.

Once we reached the relative quiet of the crowded street and the peaceful clamor of the traffic, I brought up my idea again.

"I had an idea back there. This may come as a surprise to you. Night club."

"No kidding. Inconceivable."

"You might be even more obnoxious when you can hear. I was saying we should open a place here in Manhattan where people could go to talk, and actually hear each other."

David's eyes lit up. "That's brilliant! We could soundproof the crap out of it like a recording studio and call it Quiet."

We were just getting going.

"How 'bout we dress the cocktail waitresses up like hot librarians, and . . ." I was imagining all kinds of scenarios when The Piglet burst my bubble as a true New Yorker.

"No one would go there."

"All the better," David muttered, thinking no one could hear.
But I did, and silently agreed.

* * * * *

I was shaken out of my quasi-comatose state by the wheels touching down at LAX. Ugh, reality. I thought I had become (semi) okay (ish) with my empty nest issues, but seeing The Spawn in New York had reignited my Momminess. In the excitement leading up to our visit, I hadn't prepared myself for the good-byes, and the inevitable withdrawal nosedive downward spiral that would follow.

Was I forever doomed to endure a Spawn-missing funk after every time I saw the kids?

Was this the syndrome those lamenting online empty nesters were talking about?

29
Now What?

Once Veronica and I were back in Southern California, a big realization hit. Now what? We had done everything we had set out to do. All of the people to whom we owed long-overdue visits had been duly visited. The idea of a used motor home to facilitate our travels had worked out swimmingly, and what's more, BAMF was still going strong. Our apartments were all rented out. We hadn't gone broke. Where would we go from here?

As much as Jeff kept asking us to stay longer, we all knew that his house was full and BAMF couldn't stay in his driveway forever. We had to go somewhere.

Our trip to the Big Apple was an effective reminder that the weather in most of the country had turned to full-blown winter and, after last year's Midwestern frozen frolics, neither of us wanted to go through it again. So, why not stay out in this part of the country? Spend the winter in the Desert Southwest, maybe Arizona. Yeah, that sounded like a good place to elude the cold.

I thought that some new explorations might help get Veronica's mind off of her newfound empty nest symptoms too. I could tell she was gamely fighting a big bout of separation anxiety. Christmas had been the first time we were with all three of the kids at once since the nest emptied. Leaving them definitely hit her.

So, Arizona ho—but first, I had cooked up a little surprise. Our twenty-seventh anniversary was coming right up, and I had a weird, hopefully romantic, trick up my sleeve. We could stop off in El Centro, a little town in California's Imperial Valley that retains a noteworthy place in our history. El Centro is where, after our infatuated letter-writing campaign, I made my Romeo-like return to sweep my Juliet off her feet. We stayed at the less-than-luxurious Airporter Hotel while I did five nights a week in the lounge.

After a few months, it was also where we loaded up The Shark-mobile and embarked on our trek to Nashville and an unimaginable lifetime together. All in all, I figured the sight of the place should bring back memories capable of making even the most depressed individual feel pretty nostalgic, not to mention lucky to have escaped.

At the time, even the insanity of brand-spanking-new young love couldn't immunize us from the heat, blowing sand, and outright desolation of the place. Every day we spent in El Centro, the temperature was over one hundred, topping out at a pleasant 127 one afternoon. Bare feet were impossible outdoors, air conditioners blew up daily, and we literally fried an egg in the parking lot. Yes, it can be done.

Makes it hard to believe that none of those lovely perks were the clinchers as to why we came to refer to the place as *Hell* Centro. That moniker came about when the cricket plague hit.

Millions upon millions of crickets seemed to appear overnight. I remember thinking that Pharaoh must have really pissed off God this time. The jumpy bugs covered every inch of the ground. Just walking to the hotel lobby was a disgusting exoskeleton-crunching nightmare. They came inside, under the doors and through the vents. Jumpin' jiminy! They were everywhere.

The locals took the crickets in stride; it was perfectly normal to them. They simply scooped up the insects with snow shovels. Yes, there was a thriving snow shovel business in a town where snow wouldn't have a snowball's chance in . . . never mind.

As harsh as the conditions in our little desert love nest had been, I thought those memories might cheer Veronica up. Plus, it was right on our way to wherever it was we were heading. We really didn't know, but we said our good-byes to brother Jeff and the gang, and headed east.

The feeling was quite different from our previous departures. We had no particular destination in mind beyond the next day or so. No more people left to see. Nothing on our itinerary. The plan really *was* no plans.

I let that roll around my brain while I worked my way through the freeway insanity of the Valley, LA, and San Bernardino. Finally the traffic started thinning out and I pushed BAMF up the Santa Ana Mountains that separated Los Angeles, and us, from good old Hell Centro.

30
Admitting I Have a Problem Is the First Step

Watching LA disappear in the rearview mirror, I spent all my energy holding back a crying jag. I was one "Honey, are you okay?" away from a complete breakdown.

I should have been relishing the return to our vagabond ways, but instead I felt dark and listless. The scenery whizzing by had lost its luster. David and I sat in an unusual silence. He knew better than to ask me if I was okay. He didn't need a basket case on his hands while tackling sixty-mile-an-hour, bumper-to-bumper Southern California traffic in a less-than-nimble old motor home.

As we started to climb up out of the city, I was burying myself in memories of parenthood. Focusing on the happier recollections only plunged me deeper down in the dumps, while thinking back on the harder aspects of the job gave me the guilts. Yep, I'd fallen back into full mommy-mode. I couldn't believe how much I missed my babies. My ears were actually aching from holding back tears.

Then David pierced the silence. "Oh shit!"

I caught a movement on the side of the road. A young deer, all spindly-legged and scared, was bolting from the trees and heading straight for the gap between BAMF and the vehicle ahead of us. In the heavy traffic there was nowhere to go, nothing to do but hope she would turn around. David hit the brakes and leaned on the horn while we yelled at the confused yearling to change course. Everything seemed to slow down, giving us way too much time to watch, horrified, as the fragile little fawn decided to shoot the gap in front of us. In that decelerated moment, the doomed creature looked right at me. I could taste her fear as BAMF loomed. Then the sound of her youthful body hitting the bumper and rolling underneath us restarted the clock and turned my stomach over.

I managed to hold back the urge to vomit, but not the flood of already waiting tears. David pulled over and we jumped out, but knew there was nothing to do but feel awful. Crying into David's hug, I sobbed for the little deer, and for my children who had grown up and left me behind.

David kissed the top of my head and led me back aboard. Inside, he soothed me into BAMF's loft and retook the helm so the road could rock me off to sleep.

Waking up a few hours later, snuggled in a warm cocoon of blankets, my eyes puffy from crying, I lay quietly in the semidarkness, and a calm of realization dawned. I'm supposed to be sad.

This wasn't a backslide. It's a normal, healthy process. A bout of depression after reprising my acclaimed role as mommy didn't mean I couldn't let The Spawn go; it meant that I was human. I'd actually be a freak if I could say good-bye to my children and then skip off into the sunset without a care in the world.

So I began to formulate a plan—I know, I know, the plan is no plans, but an exception was called for. The joy of seeing my babies will always have an equal and opposite reaction of separation sadness connected to it. That's an irrefutable law of nature. In the future I'd need to mentally prepare myself for the withdrawals. Plan ahead for the inevitable—and understandable—postreunion meltdown. When dealing with Spawn-visitation disengagement, I will suspend the plan-is-no-plans philosophy and envision myself steadfastly bidding farewell, and contently anticipating our next get-together.

My epiphany also clarified my vision of the new lifestyle we had embraced. It always appealed to me, perhaps stirring my ancestral gypsy heritage, but now I knew I could go forward without fear, guilt, or regret. The time had come to cast the cautions of motherhood aside and live the rest of my life.

I pulled back the curtain and peered out BAMF's loft window toward my near future, wondering what that future might be. I had no idea, but I could hardly wait. Then something looked familiar, a place I vaguely remembered from long ago.

Were we near somewhere I had lived as a kid? Did David turn around while I was asleep? I knew I recognized something about the place, but just couldn't quite conjure up what. Then I spotted the dumpy hotel by the airport on the edge of town. Oh my God, we were in Hell Centro!

31
Mexican Therapy

Our anniversary blast from the past completed, it was time to kick the plan-is-no-plans system into high gear. For the first time, Veronica and I had no real notion as to where we were going or why, other than having narrowed it down to the hundred thousand square miles or so that make up Arizona.

This new complete lack of any destination beyond the immediate changed our travel style more than we realized. It meant that we would be searching for new attractions on an almost daily basis, not just as diversions along the path to our next reunion. Our new goal was to find the interesting, enlightening, inspiring, and informative, as well as the offbeat, quirky, and unconventional, without regard to where it might take us.

So we began this new phase of our GypsyNesting by meandering around the Grand Canyon State. We had seen the big canyon years ago on a cross-country vacation with the kids, so this time we set out to find the lesser-known points of interest and found hidden gems in some remote corners of the state. Nearly every mile along the Arizona highways brought some new discovery: the ancient cliff dwellings at Tonto and Montezuma Castle National Monument, Casa Grande's giant pueblo, Organ Pipe Cactus National Park, the Petrified Forest, gunfighting at the O.K. Corral in Tombstone, the Biosphere, and even a statue *standin' on the corner* in Winslow, complete with a mural of a girl in a flatbed Ford slowing down to take a look.

Any time we ventured near the Mexican border, BAMF had a knack for attracting the Border Patrol. At one point, on a lonely stretch of two-lane in the shadow of the fence that separates us from our southern neighbor, we had three of them following us. Our encounters were always polite and professional, and we certainly appreciate and respect the difficult and dangerous job the agents are doing. The idea that our nation's southern frontier is an open, unchecked thoroughfare for illegal activities is patently absurd, and an insult to these brave men and women.

Veronica seemed to have come around and kicked the kid-missing funk that engulfed her since leaving New York. I can't say I blamed her for being blue. Saying good-bye to all three kids at once was a lot to take. I was less than jovial myself for a few days. It was the first time we had experienced that sort of unfair math.

Still, no matter how well she was dealing with her separation issues, I was totally unprepared for the bombshell she was about to drop. Something so surprising, so out of character, I thought she had to be joking.

"Let's take BAMF into Mexico."

"What?"

"Let's drive BAMF down into Mexico."

Visions of hijackings, hostage situations, and our home becoming a rolling headquarters for coyotes and drug mules danced in my head. Taking a chance like that was waaaaay out of any comfort zone of hers that I was familiar with. She had to be kidding.

"I'm not kidding."

I think the girl can actually read my mind sometimes.

Looking at the phone she added, "We've been getting Mexican cell service for the last twenty miles. There's got to be a town over the border close by."

I hemmed, and she prodded. I hawed, but she kept it up. This went on for a while, until I was convinced she wasn't faking, or testing me, or giving up. She really wanted to go. We were having a role reversal. Playing the part of the cautious pragmatist, me; and starring as the carefree adventurer . . . why, that would be my darling wife.

Finally, after usurping her famous fear-conquering mantra for myself ("people do it every day and do not die, people do it every day and do not die, people do it every day and . . ."), I gave in. Well, not completely. I agreed to drive down to a border town, on the US side, and look into it. I was pretty sure if we asked around everyone would tell us it would be crazy to drive a motor home across the border. Then we could walk across and poke around for an hour or two, maybe grab a bite, and say we'd been to Mexico.

The only crossing for miles around was at the tiny town of Gringo Pass, Arizona, across from the somewhat larger Sonoyta on the Mexican side. So we headed there to see what was what.

After parking at the gas station/store/café, otherwise known as the only place in town, I took a little stroll to scout out this lonely outpost. I found myself wishing I had spurs on 'cause the chinking sound would have accompanied the dust I was kicking up perfectly. I felt like Clint Eastwood in a spaghetti Western. In lieu of spurs, I shook my keys as each footstep landed, just in case anyone was around to hear.

Just as I was getting my Clint squint down, feeling like one tough hombre, Veronica caught up to me and broke the spell. A second later, a border patrol SUV came flying up beside us, finishing off the *High Plains Drifter* fantasy once and for all.

No big deal, we knew the routine.

"Where were you born?"

"What are you doing here?"

But this time, after the usual questions, the officer asked if we were going down to Rocky Point. We had no idea what he was talking about.

"Across the border, to Puerto Peñasco. Are you guys headed down there?"

"I don't know if that's a very good idea," was my seemingly logical reply, but then my newly unrecognizably fearless spouse jumped in.

"I really want to, but David here is a little worried. What's the deal with going across?"

Who *was* this person? She'd moved well beyond fear conquering and on to fear butt kicking.

The agent acknowledged my apprehensions, but then addressed Veronica, explaining that most of my concerns were unfounded, at least at this crossing. Our new border patrol buddy agreed there are many parts of the border that better judgment would call for avoiding, especially near the big cities like Tijuana and Juárez, but Gringo Pass wasn't one of them.

He went on to fill us in about the inviting seaside oasis just an hour or so south, Rocky Point, or Puerto Peñasco in the native tongue.

"You should go. It's great down there."

With no reason to think he was trying to send us off to meet our maker, I conceded and agreed to head on down.

Our preparations for the jaunt were minimal since, in a concerted effort to attract tourists, the Mexican government has declared about half of the state of Sonora, including Puerto Peñasco, a Hassle Free Zone. It's a bit of a strange classification, perhaps a translation twist, but it means that vehicle permits are not required within the zone, and for visits up to three days a tourist card need not be acquired.

We did purchase Mexican auto insurance though, since American policies are not recognized south of the border, and even a minor accident could become a rather large pain in the posterior without it. All traffic incidents are treated as crimes in Mexico and, as such, BAMF could be impounded and we might end up in a Mexican pokey. Coverage was available at the only place in town and only cost a few dollars a day, so there was no reason to take chances.

I'm not going to lie, we were sitting on edge as we cleared customs and navigated BAMF through the potholed, dusty streets of Sonoyta, but once we passed beyond the typical border town, the road became very nice. A newly paved thoroughfare through a lonely stretch of the Sonoran Desert. Home to lots of cactus and very few people. An hour later, we were pulling into a campground right on the beach.

Our border agent's plug for Puerto Peñasco was not the least bit overblown. The beauty of the desert meeting the ocean was stunning, the sunsets spectacular, and the waterfront stretch of the little fishing village was lined with great spots for a relaxing libation or bite overlooking the Sea of Cortez. We watched the shrimp fleet heading out in the mornings, and the dolphins heading in every afternoon. Straight-out-of-the-water fresh shrimp was delivered to BAMF's door in the evenings.

Puerto Peñasco is all about shrimp. Shrimp, shrimp and, yup, more shrimp. Bubba Gump would love Rocky Point. We ate shrimp sautéed, broiled, fried, ceviched, and relleno-ed, in enchiladas, tacos, scampi, and Mexican shrimp cocktails.

After a few afternoons of sipping mariachi-serenaded ice-cold Pacificos at sundown, it was hard to imagine how a getaway so close could have felt any farther away.

But farther away from what?

We had whiled away most of the winter. The Boy was about to finish his first year of college, and we had no idea what we were going to do. We walked the beach and talked, walked and talked. We discussed going back to Generic Midwestern College Town, moving into one of our rental units, staying near The Boy, and finding new jobs. But that would make us boomerang *parents*, and neither of us wanted that. It was highly doubtful The Boy would be too thrilled either.

We talked about finding a place in New York City, near The Piglet and Decibel. Too many people and too expensive. Not to mention, loud.

We considered some of the wonderful towns we'd seen recently. Bozeman, too cold. Tucson, too hot. Seattle, too wet. Each place was mutually struck down. At least we were in agreement. We had found the fun side of everywhere we had been, but when it came to settling somewhere, we hadn't found a home. Someday, back down to the islands, but neither of us was ready for that yet.

My formerly homebody wife, when faced with the prospect of reestablishing an abode somewhere, was genuinely disturbed. She actually said, "I'm not sure I can go back to living in one place."

In fact, I wasn't either. Neither one of us wanted to stop doing what we were doing. We had crossed a line, more than just a border. Veronica had not only grounded her helicopter, but sold it for scrap to become a risks-be-damned explorer, always looking over the horizon.

As for me, I was back on the road and feeling right at home. We had gone well past the experimental stage of travel and stumbled headlong into a completely new life. We had become perpetual motion machines.

We had to keep going. Going where? It didn't matter, just going. Going. Going Gypsy.

Epilogue

We never anticipated that a twenty-eight-year-old, $3,200 motor home purchased through eBay would last beyond the first summer, which we came to call the Summer of BAMF. By autumn we fully expected his ultimate demise at any moment. But he kept going, all the way to Mexico and the Winter of Our BAMF Content.

When it became apparent that BAMF had no intention of cashing it in, we instinctively took to following the weather, north in the summer and south for the winter, like geese.

Along the way, Veronica created a simple little website for us. Just a page to keep a small circle of friends and family abreast of our goings-on, basically a travelogue and a place to post pictures of our antics.

At some point, as we were posting accounts of our escapades, our minds went back to our initial empty nest Googling back on St. Croix. So we started voicing our opinions about empty nester life too. It may have started as a kind of digital therapy, but we figured that if we were appalled by the Alzheimer's ads and the lack of websites promoting the empty nest transition without sorrow and lamentation, there *had* to be others like us. Surely we weren't the only ones ready to embrace this new stage of our lives.

When the first one found our site and sent an email, we were thrilled, surprised, and encouraged.

> "Woo Hoo! You are my newest role models!! We are in our early to mid 40s and we have two teens (13 and 15). Of course we love them so very very much—of course we have enjoyed the wonderful years of raising them—of course we will miss them terribly when they leave—of course we look at their baby pictures wistfully and think, "Where did the time go?" BUT...We are

now in the countdown phase: 3 years with the oldest and 5 years with the youngest, then it is OUR TIME!!! The goal is to get them raised to adulthood—the goal is to teach them to BE adults who stand on their own two feet—the goal is to get to the end of the job of parenting and LET GO!!"

We were not alone.

So we stepped things up a notch and jumped into the blogosphere. Could our little family information site become an active blog? Why not? We composed our thoughts, organized our experiences, and pontificated with gusto. We even made a place for comments, and some began to trickle in.

"Love it! I am so stoked to have found your blog. I am an almost empty-nester and have started practicing so I will be ready. Till then, I can live vicariously through your awesome adventures. Rock on!!"

Yeah baby, role models and vicarious life exemplars! People were copacetic, and some of them were pretty funny:

"There's a reason teenagers are such a huge pain in the ass right before they leave—it makes it easier to let them go."

Interacting with these kindred spirits along the information superhighway made us want to seek out more of them. Waiting for people to accidentally stumble upon our unknown little blip among the millions of websites clogging cyberspace was not going to build the community of cohorts we were hoping for.

Enter The Piglet. She had been monitoring our undertaking with a growing curiosity. At some point she must have decided that we might be onto something, and she had some ideas to help us spread the message. We always knew she'd come in handy sooner or later.

She adamantly advised that we delve into the brave new world of social media. So delve we did.

We were familiar with Facebook, but it was just another place where we communicated with close family and friends. We knew it had grown beyond just a place for college kids, but we had a lot to learn. Still, at least we had some idea how to use it.

We had never even heard of the phenomenon called Twitter, much less ever dreamed of tweeting something or someone. To be honest, the whole idea of broadcasting tiny tidbits of information in 140-character tweets sounded kind of crazy. Crazy like a fox, since millions and millions are now doing it.

With some Piglet tutelage, it didn't take us long to see that there was a lot more to the social network sensation than saving on phone calls and finding old school chums. There was a whole world of people like us, restless empty nesters, ready to laugh, see the world, and love our children as adults. In short, we want to *celebrate* life after kids.

So what if our butts sag or we have hairs growing in unfortunate, unwanted places? We can still visit the world's great cities, or take off in an RV to see the next goofy attraction just around the bend. We can go back to school, volunteer to make the world a better place, or write the great American novel. We can join a roller derby team or jump out of an airplane. We can conquer our fears, and our bucket lists.

We are GypsyNesters.

* * * * *

We continue to travel the globe in constant search of new adventures. Our recent journeys include a fortnight along the Queensland coast in Australia, a month in South America and the Galapagos, a crazed ten-country Barcelona-to-Prague rental car expedition across Europe, a whirlwind foray into Central America, twenty days along Asia's Pacific Rim, a two-week cross-country Amtrak rail pass expedition, and of course, ongoing excursions across North America in BAMF.

If someday we settle somewhere, we will look back at this time as those crazy years when we lived in a state of perpetual motion.

And when we do, we'll smile.

Acknowledgments

Writing a blog and writing a book are two entirely different animals. While we had become adept at firing off quick thoughts on random topics in an Internet setting, we never could have accomplished the jump from bloggers to aspiring authors without our independent editor and mentor, **Beth Lieberman**.

From the moment we handed Beth our first draft, which probably looked like a bunch of blog posts all mashed together, she just *got us*—something for which we are forever grateful. Through her patient guidance, we learned the importance of a backstory, how to weave a consistent narrative, and that our English teachers were right: you shouldn't try to write a book without a proper outline. Once we began looking for a publisher, Beth stuck with us throughout as adviser, cheerleader, and pillar of strength. Without her counsel we would have not known how to write a book proposal, approach a publishing company, or talk about our manuscript without sounding like complete idiots. Simply stated, Beth is the best.

Then there's **Jenny Pierson**, Skyhorse editor extraordinaire. Conqueror of the comma. Master of the em dash. Tackler of tenses. Hero of the hyphen. Seriously, what editor would look at an atrocity like "if I go down in a hang gliding / bungee jumping / snowboarding / street food eating blaze of glory" and masterfully suggest "if I went down in a hang-gliding/bungee-jumping/snowboarding/street-food–eating blaze of glory" without flinching? Jenny rescued us from Unknown Writer's Purgatory, raved about us to her bosses, championed our ridiculous ideas, and still found the time to hold our hands and steady us as we took our baby steps into the publishing process. Hero of the hyphen, yes, but she is also our personal hero.

We would also like to pass along our gratitude to:

Tony Lyons for taking a chance on a crazy story like ours, and **Jay Cassell** for having faith in our manuscript.

Danielle Ceccolini for being an early *Napkin Sketch* (2013) supporter—we still can't believe it squeaked by a talent such as yourself. Anyone who can take airplane napkin stick figures scribbled by a half-asleep, brain-addled GypsyNester and turn it into the wonderful, whimsical cover it is today is Van Gogh in our eyes.

Brian Peterson for not laughing off (okay, you laughed, but in a good way) our book cover idea.

Uber-photographer **Nick Coleman** risked his life shooting our book cover photos. The fear in Veronica's eyes is not because she's falling from the nest, but that Nick might fall from the ladder on which he was precariously perched.

Christine Ragasa for her amazingly creative ideas; there's a good chance that she's the reason you're holding this book right now.

Meghan Walker, who promised to crawl through windows for us, no matter how small the opening. She proved to be more agile than we could ever have dreamed.

Sally McCartin for answering our questions, calming our fears, and making more phone calls than any human should ever be expected to.

Lauren Burnstein for putting us out there.

To the fabulous **Caitlyn Becker** for opening up her amazing wardrobe (and home) to these wandering gypsy-types. Without her, Veronica would have to show the world what living out of a suitcase *really* looks like. Also, even though she has an incredible family of her own, she graciously allows herself to be our fourth Spawn.

G-pa Larry and **Miss Kathleen** for letting us boomerang to your ranch to write our first draft. BAMF looked mighty fine parked out by your horse barn. Thanks for the nourishing muffins quietly left at our BAMF-step and allowing us into the house for your company at dinnertime.

Northern Ontario for remaining moose-less so as not to distract us while we wrote our second draft.

David's mom for her thoughtful thoughts on the manuscript. And for allowing us to turn her into a caricature that she is really not.

Michael J. Willis for maintaining his composure while we contemplated our mortality.

Yvette Grant for making us look good on the page. **Nick Grant** for pointing us in the right direction. **Bill Wolfsthal** for talking us up. And **Nicole Frail** and **Marianna Dworak**—well, you know what you did.

About the Authors

David was born in Wichita, Kansas, and grew up on the prairie and in the mountains of Colorado. He made his way in the music business as a performer, recording artist, songwriter, and radio personality in Nashville, Tennessee, and St. Croix, US Virgin Islands. After parenting and sending three kids out into the big wide world, he currently lives with his bride of thirty years, Veronica, in a state of perpetual motion.

Veronica was born and raised in Southern California and was like, totally, a Valley Girl. Against any sane person's better judgment, she ran off with a musician at age eighteen. After procreating, she became Earth Mama, then Helicopter Mom, hovering over every detail of her Spawn's lives. She has held approximately thirty-three different jobs including writer. She is never bored.